100

GREATEST FILMS

Comedy

RadioTimes

Published by
BBC Worldwide Limited
Media Centre 201 Wood Lane London W12 7TQ
ISBN13 978-0-9555886-4-8
First edition published in the United Kingdom 2009
Copyright © 2009 BBC Worldwide Limited

Publishing Director
KATHY DAY

Publisher
DAVID ROBINSON

Senior Production Co-ordinator
STEVE CALVER

Design by
STUART MANNING

Picture research by
OLIVIA HOWITT

Typesetting by
DAVID LEWIS XML ASSOCIATES LTD

Printed in Great Britain by
ANCIENT HOUSE PRESS PLC

Contents

Foreword by Andrew Collins

SIGMUND FREUD IS NOT A BARREL OF LAUGHS, but his book *Jokes and Their Relation to the Unconscious*, published over a century ago, offers a useful analysis of what makes something potentially funny. Beyond all the impenetrable stuff about "acts of ideation" and "parapraxes", he offers a list of "joke techniques", including such standbys as "diversion of a reply from the meaning of the reproach" (the comic comeback, as skilfully demonstrated in those highly verbal screwball comedies of the 1930s and 40s), "faulty reasoning" (the starting point of many a Jim Carrey farce), "the use of the absurd and nonsensical" (step forward, Mr M Python) and "multiple use of the same material" (which might go some way to explaining the appeal of the interminable parodies of the Wayans brothers).

At the end of the day, no thesis can dictate what's funny and what's not. If it makes you laugh, it's funny – end of dissertation. Which is why comedy remains the most subjective of all movie genres. One man's Arsenic is another man's Old Lace. Equally, different strains of humour suit different moods: the physical slapstick of a great silent movie by Buster Keaton, or the wordless genius of Jacques Tati, can be the perfect balm at the end of a difficult day. The same schtick can seem slight when you require material more demanding and verbal, like a Woody Allen or a Howard Hawks, or even – my favourite – the music-hall sparring in *Carry On Screaming*.

Allen, of course, managed to spin popular comedy from intellectual, literary and philosophical sources, including the work of Freud, perhaps proving that audiences aren't as dumb as the protagonists in *Dumb and Dumber*, which thankfully didn't make our 100. (Actually, the Farrelly brothers, who wrote and directed *Dumb and Dumber*, have some provocative things to say about society, but these are all too often disguised under "gross-out" sight gags, not a development that tickles me.)

When a comedy hits the spot and unites a packed auditorium in shared laughter, it is an experience to affirm life – and to lower blood pressure, release endorphins and oxygenate the body. And if the same audience is enjoying a thriller, how can you tell? They could be gripped, or asleep. The most essential part of the soundtrack to a good comedy is, uniquely, supplied by us.

Deciding on the best 100 comedy films has been no laughing matter, with fierce debate and noisy deliberation an inevitable result. But whether it's the affectionate but pin-sharp satire of *This Is Spinal Tap*, the squirming social embarrassment of *Four Weddings* or Oliver Hardy's judicious use of a mallet on Stan Laurel during their rendition of *The Trail of the Lonesome Pine* in *Way Out West*, you will find that laughter, and not the psychiatrist's couch, is actually the best medicine. ∎

Acknowledgements

REVIEWERS

ANDREW COLLINS has been the film editor of *Radio Times* since 2001. On BBC Radio 4, he presented *Back Row* and still contributes to and occasionally presents *The Film Programme*. The regular host of TCM's Short Film Awards and a former editor of *Empire* magazine, he also co-hosted ITV's *Collins & Maconie's Movie Club* with Stuart Maconie.

DAVID PARKINSON has been reviewing for *Radio Times* since 1995. Specialising in foreign-language films, he is a contributing editor on *Empire* magazine. Among his books are *A History of Film*, *Mornings in the Dark: the Graham Greene Film Reader*, *Oxford at the Movies* and *The Rough Guide to Film Musicals*.

DAVE ALDRIDGE is a former editor of *Film Review* magazine. He is currently presenter of a weekly film and DVD phone-in for BBC Radio Five Live and is a regular contributor to *Radio Times* and other entertainment magazines.

JO BERRY has written about film for publications including *Empire*, *eve*, *Maxim*, *Sight & Sound*, *The Guardian* and the *Daily Express*. She is author of *The Ultimate DVD Easter Egg Guide*, *Chick Flicks* (with Angie Errigo) and *The Parents' Guide to Kids' Movies*.

JASON CARO is a devotee of sci-fi, fantasy and thrillers, and has been a regular contributor to *Film Review* magazine as well as several specialist science-fiction publications.

JOHN FERGUSON has edited video and DVD magazines in the UK and Australia, including *Video Home Entertainment* and *Video Retailer*, most recently serving as editor of the Melbourne-based *Screen Print*. He is now based in New Zealand where he is setting up a new online DVD publication.

SLOAN FREER is an arts journalist and film critic with a passion for leftfield cinema. She has contributed to publications including *The Observer*, *Q*, *Total Film*, *Metro*, *Kerrang!* and *Bizarre*.

LORIEN HAYNES is a freelance film journalist and broadcaster, who has reviewed and interviewed for *The Observer*, *Elle*, *Red*, *Woman's Hour*, *You and Yours*, *The Green Room* and *GMTV*.

TOM HUTCHINSON, who sadly died in August 2005, contributed film reviews to *Radio Times* for a decade, and also wrote for *The Sunday Telegraph*, *The Mail on Sunday* and *Now!* magazine. A broadcaster for both radio and film, he also worked with director J Lee Thompson on several scripts, and wrote books on Marilyn Monroe and his friend Rod Steiger.

ALAN JONES has reviewed for *Radio Times* since 1995. He has written numerous TV programmes, including two documentaries on the Italian horror directors Mario Bava and Dario Argento, and is the author of *The Rough Guide to Horror Movies*.

ROBYN KARNEY is a former critic and interviewer for *Empire* magazine. Her books include *The Foreign Film Guide* with Ronald Bergan, *A Star Danced: the Life of Audrey Hepburn* and *A Singular Man: Burt Lancaster*.

STELLA PAPAMICHAEL is a freelance journalist who has reviewed films since her teens. She contributes to *Total Film* magazine and was a regular reviewer for bbc.co.uk/movies.

BRIAN PENDREIGH is a former cinema editor of *The Scotsman* and currently writes for a range of publications in the UK and overseas, including *The Times* and *Herald*. He won the Ainsworth Film Journalist of the Year award in 1995 and 1999.

TONY SLOMAN is a producer, editor and writer. His credits include *Radio On*, *Cross of Iron*, *Chitty Chitty Bang Bang* and cult TV series *The Prisoner*. A lecturer and broadcaster, he served for ten years as a governor of the BFI and is a life member of Bafta.

ADAM SMITH was deputy editor of *Empire* between 1997 and 2000, and remains the magazine's Senior Features Writer. He is also a freelance journalist and has written about movies for *Q*, *GQ*, *FHM*, *Arena*, *The Observer* and *The Independent*, and is a regular contributor to Radio 4's *Front Row*.

ADDITIONAL REVIEWERS

Leslie Felperin, Peter Freedman, Sue Heal, David McGillivray, John Marriott, David Oppedisano, Simon Rose, Adrian Turner

EDITORIAL TEAM

Edited by **SUE ROBINSON**, **COLIN PRIOR**
Contributing editor **ANDREW COLLINS**
Radio Times Film Unit **JEREMY ASPINALL**, **LUCY BARRICK**, **TOM FOLLEY**, **JAMIE HEALY**, **TONY PETERS**, **CAROLINE MARTIN**
Additional writing/research **SUSANNAH STRAUGHAN**, **ANNA RICHARDS**, **RUPERT FROST**, **PAUL BUTLER**, **STEVE MORRISSEY**, **CARI THOMAS**
Marketing by **PAUL CUMISKEY**, **TOM GUNN**
Database designed by **MARK GINNS**

PICTURE ACKNOWLEDGEMENTS

All pictures were sourced from a variety of picture libraries and suppliers, as listed below. For details of the copyright holder/s on each picture, please contact the supplier.
ALLSTAR pp1, 3, 8-16, 20, 24-28, 32, 36-44, 48-54, 58, 60, 64-72, 76-90, 94-106, 110, 112, 116-148, 152-160, 166-176, 180, 184-198, 204, 206, 209, 210a, 213, 214, 216a, 216b, 218
ANDREW COLLINS p208
GETTY pp212a, 212b
KOBAL COLLECTION pp5, 18, 22, 30, 34, 46, 62, 74, 92, 114, 150, 162, 164, 178, 182, 202, 210b, 211, 215, 217
PHOTO12 pp56, 108, 200

SOURCES

Certain data published under licence from Baseline II Inc.
Certain data published under licence from the British Board of Film Classification.
Some material is verified from the Motion Picture Guide, published by Cinebooks, New York, with kind permission.

Introduction

WELCOME TO THE RADIO TIMES 100 GREATEST FILMS SERIES, a set of books to collect and treasure that provides a lively, colourful and informative guide to *the* 100 movies in key genres. In this case, it's comedy, from silent cinema (*The General*) through to the latest critical or commercial successes (*Little Miss Sunshine*). We invite you to join us in our love of cinema, as we celebrate the best films of their kind throughout the history of the moving image, with detailed entries for each film in the 100 as well as expert analyses at the back of the book on the key influences – director, studio – in each genre. You can use these books to enhance your knowledge of film, to have fun testing your friends and family, as a starting point for your own list, or even to build a comprehensive DVD or Blu-ray library.

And how did we come up with the 100? As *Radio Times* Film Editor Andrew Collins has already mentioned in his **Foreword**, fierce debate and noisy deliberation played a major part. But the nuts and bolts of the process were that all contributors voted for their top 50, each top ten was allocated points (from 12 down to 3), with the remaining 40 getting 1 point apiece. The total was then weighted according to how many times a film had been voted for, ensuring that no one person's tastes would outweigh the majority.

Honourable mention must go to the films that almost made the 100 – but not quite. A perennial comic favourite as a TV series, *The Simpsons Movie* was only one point away, as was Russ Meyer's audacious cult hit *Beyond the Valley of the Dolls*, while the Peter Sellers satire *Being There* wasn't far behind. The **Contributors' Top Tens** section at the back of the book is marked with asterisks against titles that are not in the 100, to give you a flavour of the films that were considered but didn't make the list.

ENTRY DETAILS Every entry includes a plot synopsis and a review providing critical insights from our expert writing team (see left). ● The most memorable line from each film is quoted, with behind-the-scenes anecdotes about the film and its stars. ● We also list the essential technical details, starting with the film's British Board of Film Classification certificate (U – suitable for all; PG – parental guidance; 12, 15, 18 – passed for people of these ages and over). ● Please note that many of these films will not be suitable for family viewing, and you should be guided by the certificate and content advice when deciding on a film's suitability. ● Other details include major cast and director/writing credits. Some actors/directors are occasionally credited in different ways on different films. In these cases, we have printed the name as credited on that film, followed in square brackets by the name under which that person is more commonly known. ● The year quoted is the year the film was copyrighted. ● Its country (or countries) of origin (the nationality of its production companies, rather than where it was made) is also listed, and whether it is colour or black and white – or both, plus its running time. ● Major awards for each title (Oscars and Baftas) are also given, and any DVD extras are listed with details of the DVD edition being highlighted and Blu-ray availability.

If you have any changes that you'd like us to incorporate into the next edition of this book or any future additions to the series, please get in touch. Your contributions are invaluable, and we would be delighted to hear all your comments and suggestions. You can write to us at: Radio Times Films, BBC Worldwide Ltd, MC1D4 Media Centre, 201 Wood Lane, London W12 7TQ; or email us at films.radiotimes@bbc.co.uk.

SUE ROBINSON & **COLIN PRIOR**, SERIES EDITORS

Nicolas Cage
Meryl Streep
Chris Cooper

Directed by Spike Jonze
Screenplay by Charlie Kaufman and Donald Kaufman

Adaptation.

Adaptation.

CERTIFICATE: **15** | YEAR: **2002** | COUNTRY: **US** | **COLOUR** | RUNNING TIME: **110 MINUTES**

SYNOPSIS

As well as battling his own demons, paranoid scriptwriter Charlie Kaufman is trying to adapt challenging book *The Orchid Thief* into a scintillating screenplay. Struck by severe writer's block, he turns to his twin brother Donald for assistance, with surprising – and tragic – results.

REVIEW

Being John Malkovich director Spike Jonze again demonstrates his astonishing originality with this inventive comedy drama. Based on the Bafta-winning screenplay by Charlie Kaufman (who credits his fictitious twin brother Donald as co-writer, the first of many games Kaufman plays), the film takes the idea of life imitating art to new extremes. Instead of a straight adaptation of journalist Susan Orlean's non-fiction book *The Orchid Thief*, Jonze presents a surreal version of Kaufman turning the literary work into a screenplay. It's a dark, hilarious and visually intoxicating tale, made even more appealing by a riveting turn from Nicolas Cage as both the creatively blocked Charlie and Donald, an aspiring screenwriter of blockbusters. However, it's Meryl Streep who's the biggest revelation, adding the final brilliant touch to a dazzling and emotionally vibrant movie. **SLOAN FREER**

CAST

Nicolas Cage *Charlie Kaufman/Donald Kaufman* • Meryl Streep *Susan Orlean* • Chris Cooper *John Laroche* • Tilda Swinton *Valerie* • Cara Seymour *Amelia* • Brian Cox *Robert McKee* • Judy Greer *Alice the waitress* • Maggie Gyllenhaal *Caroline*

DIRECTOR

Spike Jonze

SCREENPLAY

Charlie Kaufman, Donald [Charlie] Kaufman, from the non-fiction book *The Orchid Thief* by Susan Orlean

AWARDS

Academy Awards (1): Supporting Actor (Chris Cooper)
Baftas (1): Adapted Screenplay

QUOTE UNQUOTE

You and I share the same DNA. Is there anything more lonely than that? **CHARLIE KAUFMAN**

IF YOU ENJOYED THIS, WHY NOT TRY . . .

Barton Fink (1991)
Being John Malkovich (1999)

■

DID YOU KNOW?

At the time of production, star Nicolas Cage and director Spike Jonze were related through marriage: Cage's cousin, director Sofia Coppola, was married to Jonze – they divorced in late 2003.

Airplane!

CERTIFICATE: **PG** | YEAR: **1980** | COUNTRY: **US** | **COLOUR** | RUNNING TIME: **84 MINUTES**

SYNOPSIS

When the eccentric passengers and crew on a flight from Los Angeles to Chicago are taken ill with food poisoning, a traumatised former air force pilot must overcome his fear of flying to land the plane. As the situation worsens, he recalls his doomed relationship with the plane's stewardess.

REVIEW

This is the first and still one of the best of Zucker, Zucker and Abrahams's wonderful movie send-ups. There's hardly a second that passes without an assault by a wickedly accurate spoof, cringe-inducing pun or inspired sight gag, and the years have not diminished the film's dumb appeal. Robert Hays and Julie Hagerty are the nominal stars, but the most fun is had by the distinguished supporting cast. It's the film that made a comedy star out of Leslie ("don't call me Shirley") Nielsen, but a whole troupe of veteran character actors – Peter Graves, Robert Stack, Lloyd Bridges, Ethel Merman (in her last film appearance) – also have a hugely enjoyable time sending up their screen personae. And, best of all, it drove a large nail into the coffin of what was becoming a very tired Hollywood institution, the *Airport* series. **JOHN FERGUSON**

CAST

Robert Hays *Ted Striker* • Julie Hagerty *Elaine Dickinson* • Leslie Nielsen *Dr Rumack* • Lloyd Bridges *McCroskey* • Robert Stack *Rex Kramer* • Kareem Abdul-Jabbar *Roger Murdock* • Peter Graves *Captain Oveur*

DIRECTOR

Jim Abrahams, David Zucker, Jerry Zucker

SCREENPLAY

Jim Abrahams, David Zucker, Jerry Zucker

DVD EXTRAS

Special Collector's Edition: commentary by Jim Abrahams, Jerry Zucker, David Zucker and Jon Davidson; deleted scenes; interviews; trivia track; theatrical trailer.

CONTENT ADVICE

Contains some swearing.

QUOTE UNQUOTE

The life of everyone on board depends upon just one thing: finding someone back there who can not only fly this plane, but who didn't have fish for dinner. **DR RUMACK**

IF YOU ENJOYED THIS, WHY NOT TRY . . .

Hellzapoppin' (1941)
The Naked Gun (1988)

DID YOU KNOW?

The movie most heavily parodied in *Airplane!* is the 1957 drama *Zero Hour*. It not only contains a character called Ted Stryker, but also includes such unintentionally hilarious lines as the "fish for dinner" quote repeated by Leslie Nielsen's doctor in the spoof.

Amélie

CERTIFICATE: **15** | YEAR: **2001** | COUNTRY: **FR/GER** | **COLOUR** | RUNNING TIME: **116 MINUTES**

SYNOPSIS

Parisian waitress Amélie Poulain discovers an old box containing a boy's lost treasures in the wall of her flat. Returning the box to its owner, she realises that her purpose in life is to make others happy and sets out to cheer up her friends and colleagues with eccentric acts of kindness.

REVIEW

Jean-Pierre Jeunet is better known as a director of nightmarish excursions into the fantastic such as *Delicatessen*, *City of Lost Children* and *Alien: Resurrection*. But this French-language romantic comedy drama enchants and beguiles with a nostalgic optimism thanks to its glorious visuals and ceaseless invention. Audrey Tautou stars as Amélie, the Montmartre waitress whose selfless *joie de vivre* leads her to improve the lives of her friends and neighbours. She only takes a break from her role of good fairy to pursue Mathieu Kassovitz, the handsome loner who collects rejected photo-booth snaps for his album of forgotten smiles. As a love letter to the City of Light – filmed at locations around Paris yet retaining the stylised magic of a movie set – this is both deliciously romantic and ingeniously mischievous. **DAVID PARKINSON**

CAST
Audrey Tautou *Amélie Poulain* • Mathieu Kassovitz *Nino Quicampoix* • Rufus *Raphaël Poulain, Amélie's father* • Yolande Moreau *Madeleine Wallace, the concierge* • Artus de Penguern *Hipolito, the writer* • Urbain Cancelier *Collignon, the grocer* • Dominique Pinon *Joseph*

DIRECTOR
Jean-Pierre Jeunet

SCREENPLAY
Guillaume Laurant, Jean-Pierre Jeunet

AWARDS
Baftas (2): Original Screenplay, Production Design

DVD EXTRAS
Two-disc Special Edition: commentary by Jean-Pierre Jeunet; interview with Jean-Pierre Jeunet; theatrical trailers; making-of featurette and cast interviews; "Script to Screen" feature; Audrey Tautou's Funny Face featurette.

QUOTE UNQUOTE
It's better to help people than garden gnomes. **AMELIE POULAIN**

IF YOU ENJOYED THIS, WHY NOT TRY . . .
Chocolat (1988)
Cinema Paradiso (1988)

DID YOU KNOW?
Jean-Pierre Jeunet cast Tautou after seeing her on a billboard of the movie *Venus Beauty Institute* in Paris near his home in Bastille.

Annie Hall

CERTIFICATE: **15** | YEAR: **1977** | COUNTRY: **US** | **COLOUR** | RUNNING TIME: **89 MINUTES**

SYNOPSIS

Successful nightclub comedian and comedy writer Alvy Singer lives alone in Manhattan, dividing his time between stage appearances, visits to the movies and sessions with his analyst. Then into his life comes Annie Hall, an insecure woman with a penchant for men's clothes and ambitions to be a singer.

REVIEW

Although Woody Allen had still to acquire great technical strength as a film-maker, this best picture Oscar winner was the movie where he found his own singular voice, a voice that echoes across events with a mixture of exuberance and introspection. Peppered with hilarious, snappy insights into the meaning of life, love, psychiatry, ambition, art and New York, this comic delight also gains considerably from the spirited playing of Diane Keaton as the titular kooky innocent from the Midwest, and Woody himself as fumbling New York neurotic Alvy Singer, a gag writer and stand-up comedian. The narrative runs parallel to the real-life relationship between the two leads in the early 1970s (Keaton's real name was Hall and she was nicknamed Annie). Future star spotters should keep an eye out for Jeff Goldblum, Beverly D'Angelo and Sigourney Weaver, who was paid a mere $50 for her six-second screen debut. **JOHN MARRIOTT**

CAST

Woody Allen *Alvy Singer* • Diane Keaton *Annie Hall* • Tony Roberts *Rob* • Carol Kane *Allison* • Paul Simon *Tony Lacey* • Shelley Duvall *Pam* • Janet Margolin *Robin* • Colleen Dewhurst *Mom Hall* • Christopher Walken *Duane Hall* • Donald Symington *Dad Hall* • Helen Ludlam *Grammy Hall* • Mordecai Lawner *Alvy's dad* • Joan Newman *Alvy's mom* • Jonathan Munk *Alvy aged nine*

DIRECTOR

Woody Allen

SCREENPLAY

Woody Allen, Marshall Brickman

AWARDS

Academy Awards (4): Film, Actress (Diane Keaton), Director, Original Screenplay
Baftas (5): Film, Actress (Diane Keaton), Director, Original Screenplay, Editing

DVD EXTRAS

Theatrical trailer.

CONTENT ADVICE

Contains swearing.

QUOTE UNQUOTE

That sex was the most fun I've ever had without laughing.
ALVY SINGER

IF YOU ENJOYED THIS, WHY NOT TRY ...

Lost in Translation (2003)
Manhattan (1979)

DID YOU KNOW?

The scene where Woody Allen sneezes into a pile of cocaine was an accident. The preview audience laughed for so long that Allen had to recut the film to make sure that the jokes that followed wouldn't be lost.

The Apartment

CERTIFICATE: **PG** | YEAR: **1960** | COUNTRY: **US** | **BW** | RUNNING TIME: **122 MINUTES**

SYNOPSIS

Spurred on by hints of salary increases and promotion, lowly insurance clerk CC Baxter loans out his apartment to the executives at his firm for their extramarital affairs. But when he falls for elevator girl Fran Kubelik, the current mistress of his boss, the arrangement becomes increasingly strained.

REVIEW

This classic from Billy Wilder cleverly veils its darker side and operates as a light romantic comedy, in which Jack Lemmon's put-upon insurance clerk offers his apartment to his married superiors so they can entertain their girlfriends. That he does it in return for promotions that never come makes "Buddy Boy" Baxter a sad case indeed. But thanks to Lemmon's skilled performance, he instantly earns our sympathy, and redemption beckons when he comes to the aid of elevator girl Shirley MacLaine, who's mistress of Lemmon's unscrupulous boss Fred MacMurray. From such potentially edgy material, Wilder and co-writer IAL Diamond (*Some Like It Hot*) sculpt an unforgettable romance that won five Oscars, including best picture (the last black-and-white movie to do so until 1993's *Schindler's List*), direction and screenplay.

ANDREW COLLINS

CAST

Jack Lemmon *CC "Bud" Baxter* • Shirley MacLaine *Fran Kubelik* • Fred MacMurray *JD Sheldrake* • Ray Walston *Mr Dobisch* • David Lewis *Mr Kirkeby* • Jack Kruschen *Dr Dreyfuss* • Joan Shawlee *Sylvia* • Edie Adams *Miss Olsen* • Hope Holiday *Margie MacDougall*

DIRECTOR

Billy Wilder

SCREENPLAY

Billy Wilder, IAL Diamond

AWARDS

Academy Awards (5): Film, Director, Original Screenplay, Art Direction, Editing
Baftas (3): Film, Foreign Actor (Jack Lemmon), Foreign Actress (Shirley MacLaine)

DVD EXTRAS

Theatrical trailer.

QUOTE UNQUOTE

When you're in love with a married man, you shouldn't wear mascara. **FRAN KUBELIK**

IF YOU ENJOYED THIS, WHY NOT TRY...

How to Succeed in Business without Really Trying (1967)
The Seven Year Itch (1955)

DID YOU KNOW?

Billy Wilder definitely had something about the name Sheldrake. Not only does Fred MacMurray's adulterous boss here go by the name, but it was also used in Wilder's *Ace in the Hole*, *Sunset Blvd* and *Kiss Me Stupid*.

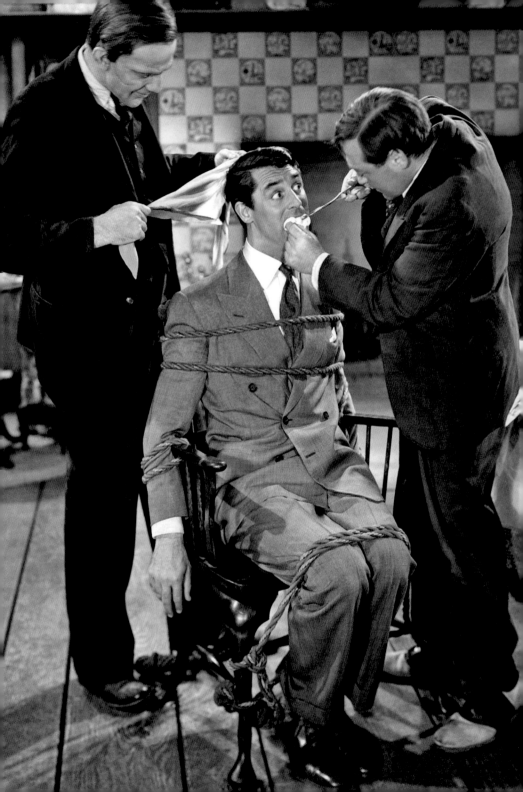

Arsenic and Old Lace

CERTIFICATE: **PG** | YEAR: **1944** | COUNTRY: **US** | **BW** | RUNNING TIME: **113 MINUTES**

SYNOPSIS

Doting nephew Mortimer Brewster is visiting his seemingly respectable maiden aunts Abby and Martha on Halloween when he makes a shocking discovery – the outwardly sweet old ladies are poisoning the lonely gentlemen who lodge in their Brooklyn house, and burying them in the basement.

REVIEW

From the moment he saw Joseph Kesselring's hit play, Frank Capra was determined to bring this frantic comedy to the screen. Although forced to settle for Raymond Massey after he failed to get Boris Karloff to repeat his stage triumph as the nasty nephew (Jonathan Brewster), Capra was blessed with a sparkling cast. Cary Grant only agreed to take the lead as it gave him the chance to reunite with Jean Adair, who had once nursed him through a nasty bout of rheumatic fever, but he gives one of his most unguarded performances, hurling himself into the part of the decent nephew who discovers that his respectable aunts (played with hilarious dottiness by Adair and Josephine Hull) are serial killers. Spookily lit and very funny, the film is unmissable, with Grant's wonderful double-takes giving the action the farcical element needed to lighten the pitch-black humour. **DAVID PARKINSON**

CAST

Cary Grant *Mortimer Brewster* • Priscilla Lane *Elaine Harper* • Raymond Massey *Jonathan Brewster* • Jack Carson *O'Hara* • Edward Everett Horton *Mr Witherspoon* • Peter Lorre *Dr Einstein* • James Gleason *Lt Rooney* • Josephine Hull *Abby Brewster* • Jean Adair *Martha Brewster* • John Alexander *"Teddy Roosevelt" Brewster* • Grant Mitchell *Reverend Harper* • Edward McNamara *Brophy* • Garry Owen *Taxi cab driver*

DIRECTOR

Frank Capra

SCREENPLAY

Julius J & Philip G Epstein, from the play by Joseph Kesselring

DVD EXTRAS

Theatrical trailer.

QUOTE UNQUOTE

For a gallon of elderberry wine, I take one teaspoon full of arsenic, then add half a teaspoon full of strychnine, and then just a pinch of cyanide. **AUNT MARTHA**

IF YOU ENJOYED THIS, WHY NOT TRY . . .

The Cat and the Canary (1939)
The Last Supper (1995)

■

DID YOU KNOW?

During a scene in a graveyard, Cary Grant sits on a tomb near a headstone bearing his real name – Archie Leach.

Austin Powers: International Man of Mystery

CERTIFICATE: **15** | YEAR: **1997** | COUNTRY: **US** | **COLOUR** | RUNNING TIME: **90 MINUTES**

SYNOPSIS

Cryogenically preserved since the 1960s, British super-agent Austin Powers emerges from self-imposed hibernation to do battle with his arch nemesis, Dr Evil, who is threatening world domination. But Austin discovers that many of his attitudes have dated badly during his 30 years in the deep freeze.

REVIEW

This Swinging Sixties spy spoof is a fast, furious and fabulously funny ride that expertly mocks every groovy fad, psychedelic fashion and musical style of the period. Mike Myers is brilliant as the secret agent-cum-fashion photographer, cryogenically frozen so he can foil the plans of his arch nemesis, Dr Evil (Myers again), in the 1990s. Witty, sophisticated and hysterically stupid by turns, the side-splitting humour arises from clever culture-clash comedy (free love versus safe sex), knockabout farce, Austin's catchphrases – "Oh, behave!" – and countless references to 007, Matt Helm and *Our Man Flint*. Elizabeth Hurley is fantastic as ersatz Bond girl Vanessa Kensington, and there are memorable cameos from Rob Lowe, Christian Slater and Will Ferrell in one of his first movie appearances. Two sequels followed, but failed to top this shagadelic original. **ALAN JONES**

QUOTE UNQUOTE

As long as people are still having promiscuous sex with many anonymous partners without protection while at the same time experimenting with mind-expanding drugs... I'll be sound as a pound. **AUSTIN POWERS**

IF YOU ENJOYED THIS, WHY NOT TRY . . .

Austin Powers: the Spy Who Shagged Me (1999)
Our Man Flint (1966)

CAST

Mike Myers *Austin Powers/Dr Evil* • Elizabeth Hurley *Vanessa Kensington* • Michael York *Basil Exposition* • Mimi Rogers *Mrs Kensington* • Robert Wagner *Number Two* • Seth Green *Scott Evil* • Fabiana Udenio *Alotta Fagina* • Mindy Sterling *Frau Farbissina* • Burt Bacharach

DIRECTOR

Jay Roach

SCREENPLAY

Mike Myers

DVD EXTRAS

Commentary by Mike Myers and Jay Roach; deleted scenes, including two alternative endings; cast biographies and filmographies; cameo menu. Also available on Blu-ray.

CONTENT ADVICE

Contains swearing, nudity.

DID YOU KNOW?

Mike Meyers had three sets of false teeth made for the film, in order to achieve different facial effects.

The Awful Truth

CERTIFICATE: **U** | YEAR: **1937** | COUNTRY: **US** | **BW** | RUNNING TIME: **87 MINUTES**

SYNOPSIS

When Jerry Warriner can't explain the Florida vacation he didn't spend in Florida and his wife fails to convince him her night away from home was because of a broken-down car, the suspicious couple begin divorce proceedings. But, try as they might, they can't resist the urge to see each other.

REVIEW

This is a wonderful example of Cary Grant at his screwball comic best, playing one half of a sniping, divorcing couple, who trade insults like gunfire and seek to spoil each other's future plans. Irene Dunne is the superb foil for Grant's laconic asides, bringing a wonderful sense of mischief to the role of possibly wronged but perhaps not entirely innocent wife. It's no wonder their separation proves almost as much of a trial as their marriage, as the pair spark beautifully off each other. Grant and Dunne are assisted by a great supporting cast, which includes Ralph Bellamy and Cecil Cunningham, and Leo McCarey's assured and fluid direction was rightly rewarded with an Oscar. Many stars, including Tom Hanks and Hugh Grant, have laid claim to Grant's mantle, but this movie illustrates once again that they are light years away from the man at his best. **SUE HEAL**

CAST

Irene Dunne *Lucy Warriner* • Cary Grant *Jerry Warriner* • Ralph Bellamy *Daniel Leeson* • Alexander D'Arcy [Alex D'Arcy] *Armand Duvalle* • Cecil Cunningham *Aunt Patsy* • Molly Lamont *Barbara Vance* • Esther Dale *Mrs Leeson* • Joyce Compton *Dixie Belle Lee/Toots Binswanger*

DIRECTOR

Leo McCarey

SCREENPLAY

Viña Delmar [Vina Delmar], from the play by Arthur Richman

AWARDS

Academy Awards (1): Director

QUOTE UNQUOTE

Well, I'm gonna be tanned and Lucy's not gonna be embarrassed. And what wives don't know won't hurt them.
JERRY WARRINER

IF YOU ENJOYED THIS, WHY NOT TRY ...

Let's Do It Again (1953)
My Favorite Wife (1940)

DID YOU KNOW?

The film was adapted from a Broadway play that ran for over 100 performances in the early 1920s. It first became a film in 1925 and then again in 1929, with Jane Wyman and Ray Milland revisiting the story in 1953 in *Let's Do It Again*.

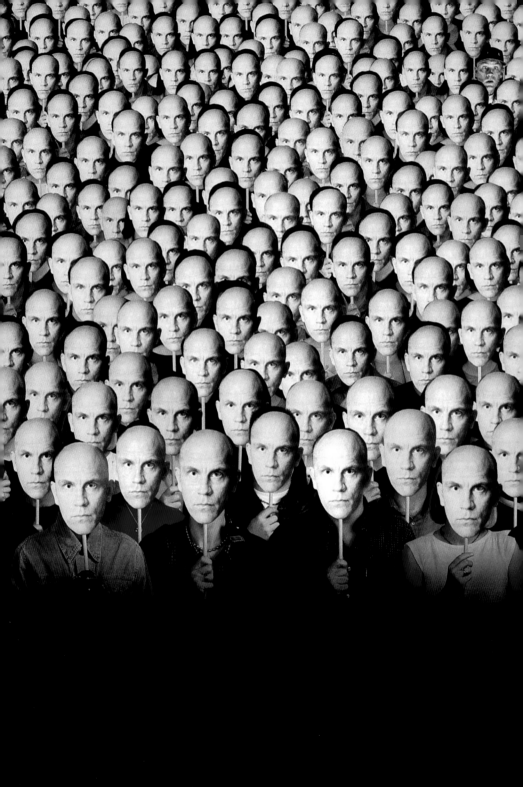

Being John Malkovich

CERTIFICATE: **15** | YEAR: **1999** | COUNTRY: **US** | **COLOUR** | RUNNING TIME: **108 MINUTES**

SYNOPSIS

Impoverished puppeteer Craig Schwartz takes a job at a strange firm situated on floor 7½ of an office block, where a small door reveals a tunnel leading into the head of John Malkovich. Craig and co-worker Maxine decide to offer New Yorkers the chance to be the actor for 15 minutes.

REVIEW

This crazy, surreal Bafta-winning comedy from director Spike Jonze (*Adaptation.*) consistently dazzles while never losing its grip on unreality. It's a daringly original metaphysical fantasy that still finds time to ponder the human status quo, sexual gender and identity, as puppeteer John Cusack finds a door leading into John Malkovich's head. Super-smart, hip and darkly subversive, Jonze's Kafkaesque mind trip is so far-out in conservative Hollywood terms, it's a real shock to the system. Who else would consider casting Cameron Diaz as a dowdy, animal-obsessed wife? And the sequence where Malkovich enters his own brain portal and finds a world completely populated by images of himself is a classic of extraordinary imagination. The fact that it manages to carry its open-mouthed audience through every awesomely enigmatic turn is its greatest accomplishment. **ALAN JONES**

CAST

John Cusack *Craig Schwartz* • Catherine Keener *Maxine* • Cameron Diaz *Lotte Schwartz* • John Malkovich *John Horatio Malkovich* • Orson Bean *Dr Lester* • Mary Kay Place *Floris* • Carlos Jacott *Larry the agent* • Charlie Sheen *Charlie* • Brad Pitt • Sean Penn

DIRECTOR

Spike Jonze

SCREENPLAY

Charlie Kaufman

AWARDS

Baftas (1): Original Screenplay

DVD EXTRAS

Cast and crew filmographies and biographies; *American Arts and Culture Presents: John Horatio Malkovich, Dance of Despair and Disillusionment, Art of Puppeteering* and *Art of Background Diving* featurettes; *7½ Floor Orientation*; Spike Jonze interview; TV spots; photo album; theatrical trailer.

CONTENT ADVICE

Contains swearing, sex scenes.

QUOTE UNQUOTE

Do you know what a metaphysical can of worms this portal is? **CRAIG SCHWARTZ**

IF YOU ENJOYED THIS, WHY NOT TRY . . .

Adaptation. (2002)
How to Get Ahead in Advertising (1989)

DID YOU KNOW?

When John Malkovich first read Charlie Kaufman's script, his reaction was "Why does this guy hate me?"

Best in Show

CERTIFICATE: **12** | YEAR: **2000** | COUNTRY: **US** | **COLOUR** | RUNNING TIME: **86 MINUTES**

SYNOPSIS

At the prestigious Mayflower Dog Show in Philadelphia, the tension is building and the spotlight is on the owners of five prize pooches: a pair of neurotic yuppies, a trophy wife and her handler, a bubbly gay couple, a soulful bait-shop owner and a woman with a past married to a guy with two left feet.

REVIEW

After lampooning a heavy metal band in *This Is Spinal Tap* and amateur dramatics in *Waiting for Guffman*, "mockumentary" maestro Christopher Guest scores again with this howlingly funny look at dog owners. Guest co-writes, directs and appears in this sharp but never malicious satire that follows a cross section of contestants preparing for a (fictitious) Philadelphia dog show. Playing breeders who are often more highly strung than their pets, the members of the impeccable ensemble cast improvise their way through an inspired series of keenly observed set pieces. Guest, Michael McKean, Catherine O'Hara and Eugene Levy all hit the spot, but the standout is Fred Willard, whose badly briefed TV compere is a masterly creation. Eschewing cheap shots, yet not afraid of outrageous caricature, this is laugh-out-loud comedy with pedigree and bite.

DAVID PARKINSON

CAST

Christopher Guest *Harlan Pepper* • Eugene Levy *Gerry Fleck* • Catherine O'Hara *Cookie Fleck* • Michael McKean *Stefan Vanderhoof* • John Michael Higgins *Scott Donlan* • Fred Willard *Buck Laughlin* • Jennifer Coolidge *Sherri Ann Ward Cabot* • Jane Lynch *Christy Cummings* • Parker Posey *Meg Swan* • Michael Hitchcock *Hamilton Swan* • Bob Balaban *Dr Theodore W Millbank III*

DIRECTOR

Christopher Guest

SCREENPLAY

Christopher Guest, Eugene Levy

DVD EXTRAS

Commentary by Christopher Guest and Eugene Levy; deleted scenes with optional commentary by Christopher Guest and Eugene Levy; theatrical trailer.

CONTENT ADVICE

Contains some swearing.

QUOTE UNQUOTE

And to think that in some countries these dogs are eaten.

BUCK LAUGHLIN

IF YOU ENJOYED THIS, WHY NOT TRY ...

For Your Consideration (2006)
Waiting for Guffman (1996)

DID YOU KNOW?

The bloodhound's name, Hubert, is derived from the Gallic name for a bloodhound – the French call it a Saint Hubert.

Big

CERTIFICATE: **12** | YEAR: **1988** | COUNTRY: **US** | **COLOUR** | RUNNING TIME: **99 MINUTES**

SYNOPSIS

At a fairground fortune-telling booth, a 12-year-old boy wishes that he could be "big". The next morning, he is astonished to find himself transformed into a full-grown man. Afraid and isolated, he realises that only his best friend will believe what's happened, and together they head for the big city.

REVIEW

Tom Hanks received his first Academy Award nomination for his fine performance in this goofy comedy (he made up for not winning by being awarded consecutive best actor Oscars – for *Philadelphia* and *Forrest Gump* – in the 1990s). He plays a 12-year-old boy transplanted by a carnival wishing contraption ("I wish I were big.") into a man's body, and his portrayal of a simple but sincere guy in a cynical world foreshadows his role as Gump. Elizabeth Perkins also makes an impact as a co-worker who finds herself strangely attracted to Hanks's little big man. *Big* may well be a formula fantasy movie, but Penny Marshall's polished direction combined with Hanks's gauche charm make it the best of the spate of body-swap movies turned out by Hollywood in the late 1980s.

PETER FREEDMAN

CAST

Tom Hanks *Josh Baskin* • Elizabeth Perkins *Susan Lawrence* • Robert Loggia *"Mac" MacMillan* • John Heard *Paul Davenport* • Jared Rushton *Billy Kopeche* • David Moscow *Young Josh* • Jon Lovitz *Scotty Brennen* • Mercedes Ruehl *Mrs Baskin* • Josh Clark *Mr Baskin*

DIRECTOR

Penny Marshall

SCREENPLAY

Gary Ross, Anne Spielberg

DVD EXTRAS

Special Edition: theatrical version of the film and extended version; commentary by Gary Rose and Anne Spielberg; deleted scenes with introductions by Penny Marshall; five featurettes; theatrical trailers; TV spots.

CONTENT ADVICE

Contains swearing.

QUOTE UNQUOTE

You're Josh Baskin, remember? You broke your arm on my roof. You hid in my basement when Robert Dyson was about to rip your head off... **BILLY**

IF YOU ENJOYED THIS, WHY NOT TRY . . .

Freaky Friday (1976)
13 Going on 30 (2004)

DID YOU KNOW?

Tom Hanks nearly didn't get the lead – or his first Oscar nomination – in Penny Marshall's body-swap comedy. It almost went to Harrison Ford, with Steven Spielberg (whose sister co-wrote the screenplay) slated to direct.

The Big Lebowski

CERTIFICATE: **18** | YEAR: **1997** | COUNTRY: **US/UK** | **COLOUR** | RUNNING TIME: **112 MINUTES**

SYNOPSIS

Unemployed hippy Jeff "the Dude" Lebowski is attacked in his apartment by two thugs who mistake him for a millionaire with the same surname. Looking for some compensation for his ruined rug, "the Dude" decides to pay the original intended victim a visit, with surprising results.

REVIEW

Like the best of their work, the Coen brothers' goofy tribute to Raymond Chandler and *film noir* (particularly *The Big Sleep*) is packed with great lines, ingenious plot twists and eccentric characters. There are, in fact, two Lebowskis: one is Jeff Bridges, who calls himself "the Dude", an ageing hippy who becomes embroiled in the kidnapping of the other Lebowski's young wife, aided and abetted by tenpin bowling chum John Goodman. What follows is an insane labyrinth of a plot that encompasses the drug and porn underworlds, Busby Berkeley fantasies and bath time with a savage marmot. It's a distinctive, crazy treat, decked out with a trademark moody thriller narration and marvellous performances from Bridges, the toothsome and taciturn Steve Buscemi, and Coen regular Goodman, who based his Vietnam-veteran character on the bear-like writer/director John Milius. **ADRIAN TURNER**

QUOTE UNQUOTE

I'm the Dude. So that's what you call me. You know, that or, uh, His Dudeness, or uh, Duder, or El Duderino if you're not into the whole brevity thing. **JEFF "THE DUDE" LEBOWSKI**

IF YOU ENJOYED THIS, WHY NOT TRY ...

The Big Sleep (1946)
Gumshoe (1971)

■

CAST

Jeff Bridges *Jeff "The Dude" Lebowski* • John Goodman *Walter Sobchak* • Julianne Moore *Maude Lebowski* • Steve Buscemi *Donny* • David Huddleston *The Big Lebowski* • Philip Seymour Hoffman *Brandt* • John Turturro *Jesus Quintana* • Tara Reid *Bunny Lebowski*

DIRECTOR

Joel Coen

SCREENPLAY

Ethan Coen, Joel Coen

DVD EXTRAS

Special Edition: making-of documentary; spoof introduction; Jeff Bridges photography; production notes.

CONTENT ADVICE

Contains drug abuse, violence, swearing.

DID YOU KNOW?

The jersey featuring a Japanese baseball player worn by Jeff Bridges in the film is his own and also makes an appearance in *The Fisher King*.

Bill & Ted's Excellent Adventure

CERTIFICATE: **PG** | YEAR: **1988** | COUNTRY: **US** | **COLOUR** | RUNNING TIME: **86 MINUTES**

SYNOPSIS

California teenagers Bill and Ted are eager to succeed in a history exam because failure will result in Ted being sent to military school, ending the duo's hopes of becoming rock stars. Then a representative from the future arrives and assists their studies by enabling them to travel back in time.

REVIEW

A nonstop giggle from start to finish, this beguiling grab-bag of time-travel clichés, hard-rock music and Valley-speaking dudes is a flawless, purpose-built junk movie. Director Stephen Herek's scattershot style perfectly complements the wayward cosmic capers, as air-guitar playing airheads Keanu Reeves and Alex Winter plunder history for the great and the good to avoid flunking school. Among the many highlights are Bill & Ted's short-lived glee at being sentenced to a medieval iron maiden, Napoleon's childish tantrums at a bowling alley, plus a running gag about Bill's inappropriately young stepmother. A pre-sex symbol Reeves is particularly good value, resembling a moronic puppet with loose strings ambling amiably through his happy-go-lucky voyage, and he and Winter reteamed in 1991 for the inevitable but still satisfying sequel *Bill & Ted's Bogus Journey*. **ALAN JONES**

CAST

Keanu Reeves *Ted "Theodore" Logan* • Alex Winter *Bill S Preston* • George Carlin *Rufus* • Terry Camilleri *Napoleon* • Dan Shor *Billy the Kid* • Tony Steedman *Socrates* • Rod Loomis *Sigmund Freud* • Al Leong *Genghis Khan* • Jane Wiedlin *Joan of Arc*

DIRECTOR

Stephen Herek

SCREENPLAY

Chris Matheson, Ed Solomon

DVD EXTRAS

Theatrical trailer; photo gallery.

CONTENT ADVICE

Contains swearing.

QUOTE UNQUOTE

Excellent! BILL & TED

IF YOU ENJOYED THIS, WHY NOT TRY ...

Bill & Ted's Bogus Journey (1991)
Wayne's World (1992)

DID YOU KNOW?

Napoleon's battle campaign was made to look realistically epic by using actual footage from the 1956 adaptation of *War and Peace*.

Billy Liar

CERTIFICATE: **PG** | YEAR: **1963** | COUNTRY: **UK** | **BW** | RUNNING TIME: **94 MINUTES**

SYNOPSIS

Billy Fisher is an ambitious, decidedly creative but lazy young man who lives with his parents in an unexciting northern town. Bored by his job as a clerk in an undertaker's office, he retreats into a world of fantasy and lies, much to the annoyance of his family, his bosses and his fiancées.

REVIEW

A bestselling novel and a smash-hit stage play, Keith Waterhouse and Willis Hall's *Billy Liar* was brought to the screen by director John Schlesinger as a faultless blend of social realism and satirical fantasy. Tom Courtenay gives one of the best performances of his career as the day-dreaming undertaker's assistant who escapes from his mundane existence in a grey northern town into the neverland of Ambrosia, where he is supreme dictator. The performances around him are all first rate, notably Julie Christie and Helen Fraser as two of the three women in his life, Wilfred Pickles and Mona Washbourne as his long-suffering parents, and Leonard Rossiter as his humourless boss, Shadrack. This gem of the British New Wave is a must-see, though please be warned that the casually expressed racism is very much of its time. **DAVID PARKINSON**

CAST

Tom Courtenay *Billy Fisher* • Julie Christie *Liz* • Wilfred Pickles *Geoffrey Fisher* • Mona Washbourne *Alice Fisher* • Ethel Griffies *Florence, grandmother* • Finlay Currie *Duxbury* • Rodney Bewes *Arthur Crabtree* • Helen Fraser *Barbara* • Leonard Rossiter *Shadrack*

DIRECTOR

John Schlesinger

SCREENPLAY

Keith Waterhouse, Willis Hall, from their play and the novel by Keith Waterhouse

QUOTE UNQUOTE

Today's a day of big decisions. Going to start writing me novel – 2,000 words every day – going to start getting up in the morning. **BILLY FISHER**

IF YOU ENJOYED THIS, WHY NOT TRY . . .

Hail the Conquering Hero (1944)
The Secret Life of Walter Mitty (1947)

DID YOU KNOW?

Billy Liar was also made into an ITV sitcom in the mid-1970s, with Jeff Rawle (Amos Diggory in *Harry Potter and the Goblet of Fire*) in the title role.

Blazing Saddles

CERTIFICATE: **15** | YEAR: **1974** | COUNTRY: **US** | **COLOUR** | RUNNING TIME: **88 MINUTES**

SYNOPSIS

When black railway worker Bart is made sheriff of Rock Ridge, it seems like a great opportunity to fight prejudice and corruption. Little does he know that his appointment is part of the land-grabbing scheme of speculator Hedley Lamarr. But help is at hand from the once legendary "Waco Kid".

REVIEW

This all-singing, all-belching western spoof remains one of writer/director Mel Brooks's finest creations. Cleavon Little stars as the smart-as-a-whip railway worker who is appointed the first black sheriff to a hell-raising western town; Gene Wilder plays the Waco Kid, the drunken gunman who helps him out. The two stars are great together, but there are even better performances from Madeline Kahn as Lili Von Shtupp (sending up Marlene Dietrich in an Oscar-nominated performance), former American football star Alex Karras as dumb strongman Mongo and the crazed Harvey Korman as slimy villain Hedley (not Hedy!) Lamarr. Brooks also turns up as the easily swayed Governor Le Petomane. There's not a lot of subtlety here, but loads of slapstick and more jokes about bodily functions than you'll find in the average contemporary gross-out movie.

JOHN FERGUSON

CAST

Cleavon Little *Bart* • Gene Wilder *Jim, the Waco Kid* • Slim Pickens *Taggart* • Harvey Korman *Hedley Lamarr* • Madeline Kahn *Lili Von Shtupp* • Mel Brooks *Governor Le Petomane/Indian chief* • David Huddleston *Olson Johnson* • Liam Dunn *Rev Johnson* • Alex Karras *Mongo*

DIRECTOR

Mel Brooks

SCREENPLAY

Mel Brooks, Norman Steinberg, Andrew Bergman, Richard Pryor, Alan Uger, from a story by Bergman

DVD EXTRAS

30th Anniversary Edition: commentary by Mel Brooks; featurette on Madeline Kahn; additional scenes; *Back in the Saddle* cast and crew reunion documentary; *Black Bart* – 1975 TV pilot; theatrical trailer. Also available on Blu-ray.

CONTENT ADVICE

Contains swearing.

QUOTE UNQUOTE

Hello, handsome, is that a ten-gallon hat or are you just enjoying the show? LILI VON SHTUPP

IF YOU ENJOYED THIS, WHY NOT TRY . . .

Son of Paleface (1952)
Support Your Local Sheriff! (1969)

DID YOU KNOW?

After bumping into John Wayne at Warner Bros studios, Mel Brooks offered the legendary star a part in the movie and gave him the script. But The Duke refused the role graciously, saying "I'll be first in line to see it."

The Blues Brothers

CERTIFICATE: **15** | YEAR: **1980** | COUNTRY: **US** | **COLOUR** | RUNNING TIME: **127 MINUTES**

SYNOPSIS

After Elwood Blues collects his brother Jake from jail, they learn that their old Catholic orphanage has only 11 days to find $5,000 in taxes, or close. They resolve to get their band back together for a gig to raise the money, but their "mission from God" attracts as many enemies as fans.

REVIEW

This wonderful sprawling mess of a movie remains one of the best musical comedies of modern times. Born out of star/co-writer Dan Aykroyd's abiding love of soul and blues music, the story sees him and John Belushi resurrecting their old band (which includes luminaries such as Booker T and the MGs members Steve Cropper and Donald Dunn). It's the skimpiest of plots that's really just an excuse for a string of rousing musical numbers and cameo appearances from music legends such as Aretha Franklin, Cab Calloway and Ray Charles. In between the songs, director John Landis gathers an increasingly manic group of characters, including a rabid country-and-western band, a bunch of neo-Nazis and Belushi's vengeful former lover (a wonderful Carrie Fisher), who join the massed forces of law and order in a ludicrously spectacular car chase. **JOHN FERGUSON**

CAST

John Belushi *"Joliet" Jake Blues* • Dan Aykroyd *Elwood Blues* • Kathleen Freeman *Sister Mary Stigmata* • James Brown *Reverend Cleophus James* • Cab Calloway *Curtis* • Carrie Fisher *Mystery woman* • Ray Charles *Ray* • Aretha Franklin *Soul Food Cafe owner* • John Candy *Burton Mercer* • Henry Gibson *Nazi leader* • Steven Spielberg *Cook county clerk* • Twiggy *Chic lady* • Paul Reubens *Waiter*

DIRECTOR

John Landis

SCREENPLAY

John Landis, Dan Aykroyd

DVD EXTRAS

Extended version of the film; making-of feature; production notes, cast and film-maker biographies; introduction by Dan Aykroyd; musical highlights; transposing the music; "Remembering John" feature. Also available on Blu-ray.

CONTENT ADVICE

Contains swearing.

QUOTE UNQUOTE

It's got a cop motor, a 440 cubic inch plant, it's got cop tires, cop suspensions, cop shocks. It's a model made before catalytic converters so it'll run good on regular gas. ...is it the new Bluesmobile or what? **ELLWOOD**

IF YOU ENJOYED THIS, WHY NOT TRY . . .

National Lampoon's Animal House (1978)
1941 (1979)

■

DID YOU KNOW?

Renowned for its proliferation of car crashes, this film held the world record for the number of vehicles written off during a movie.

Borat: Cultural Learnings of America for Make Benefit Glorious Nation of Kazakhstan

CERTIFICATE: **15** | YEAR: **2006** | COUNTRY: **US/UK** | **COLOUR** | RUNNING TIME: **80 MINUTES**

SYNOPSIS

The sixth best-known reporter in Kazakhstan "investigates" America, causing no end of chaos and offence along the way. The innocent abroad is a little distracted by his secondary mission to meet Pamela Anderson, but still manages to air his breathtaking attitudes to race, religion and gender.

REVIEW

For those unfamiliar with Borat, he is a leading Kazakhstani journalist who, for this project, travels America learning about its culture. He is also a complete fabrication, the work of Ali G creator Sacha Baron Cohen. Thus his scatologically uproarious investigation includes a scene in which he attends a posh dinner party and returns from the bathroom with his excrement in a plastic bag. He also destroys a Civil War memorabilia shop and lets loose a chicken on the New York subway. A minor niggle is that at least a handful of the sequences might have been set up to some degree. And in cinematic terms it is absolutely nothing special: there's no real reason for it to be a movie at all – its natural home may well be on DVD. But as an example of a comedian willing to take absurd risks for his art, this film – one of the funniest of 2006 – will probably never be surpassed. **ADAM SMITH**

QUOTE UNQUOTE

My name is Borat, I come e-from Kazakhastan. Can I say e-first, we support your "War of Terror". **BORAT**

IF YOU ENJOYED THIS, WHY NOT TRY...

Brüno (2009)
Roger & Me (1989)

∎

CAST

Sacha Baron Cohen *Borat Sagdiyev* • Ken Davitian *Azamat Bagatov* • Luenell • Pamela Anderson

DIRECTOR

Larry Charles

SCREENPLAY

Sacha Baron Cohen, Anthony Hines, Peter Baynham, Dan Mazer, from a story by Baron Cohen, Hines, Baynham, Todd Phillips, from the character created by Baron Cohen

DVD EXTRAS

Kazakh police warning video; two theatrical trailers; deleted scenes; *Baywatch* spoof; rodeo news report; promotional tour and premiere footage; Borat infomercial.

CONTENT ADVICE

Contains swearing, sexual references.

DID YOU KNOW?

Sacha Baron Cohen doesn't speak "Kazakh" in the film – it's just Hebrew with a supposedly east-European accent.

Bringing Up Baby

CERTIFICATE: **U** | YEAR: **1938** | COUNTRY: **US** | **BW** | RUNNING TIME: **102 MINUTES**

SYNOPSIS

David Huxley is a quiet academic, dedicated to zoological research. He is perfectly content to live out his life among the dry bones of prehistoric dinosaurs. But when he encounters society girl Susan Vance and her pet leopard Baby, his peaceful life is shattered and a madcap adventure begins.

REVIEW

How sublime can movies get? This shimmering dissection of the male-female relationship is perfectly cast (Katharine Hepburn in a celebrated screwball role accompanied by pet leopard), brilliantly written by Hagar Wilde and *Stagecoach's* Dudley Nichols and fabulously directed by Howard Hawks. It's a genuinely funny original that repays repeated viewings, especially to marvel at the variety of subtle expressions on the face of "Professor" Cary Grant, who gives one of the most wonderful comic performances ever to grace the silver screen. He's the shy palaeontologist whose search for funding brings him into Hepburn's sights. She pursues him with manic determination, throwing his life and career into chaos. Regarded as too wacky by half on first release, it's now widely considered a classic, and rightly so. **TONY SLOMAN**

CAST

Katharine Hepburn *Susan Vance* • Cary Grant *Dr David Huxley* • Charlie Ruggles [Charles Ruggles] *Major Horace Applegate* • Walter Catlett *Constable Slocum* • Barry Fitzgerald *Mr Gogarty* • May Robson *Mrs Carleton Random, Aunt Elizabeth* • Fritz Feld *Dr Fritz Lehmann* • Leona Roberts *Mrs Hannah Gogarty* • George Irving *Mr Alexander Peabody* • Tala Birell *Mrs Lehmann* • Virginia Walker *Alice Swallow*

DIRECTOR

Howard Hawks

SCREENPLAY

Dudley Nichols, Hagar Wilde, from a short story by Wilde in *Collier's*

QUOTE UNQUOTE

Now it isn't that I don't like you, Susan, because, after all, in moments of quiet, I'm strangely drawn toward you, but – well, there haven't been any quiet moments. **DAVID HUXLEY**

IF YOU ENJOYED THIS, WHY NOT TRY ...

Monkey Business (1952)
A Private Function (1984)

DID YOU KNOW?

If you think Asta in *The Thin Man* and George in *Bringing Up Baby* look similar, it's because they're played by the same dog – a wire-haired terrier aptly named Skippy. At the height of his career the dog commanded $250 per week.

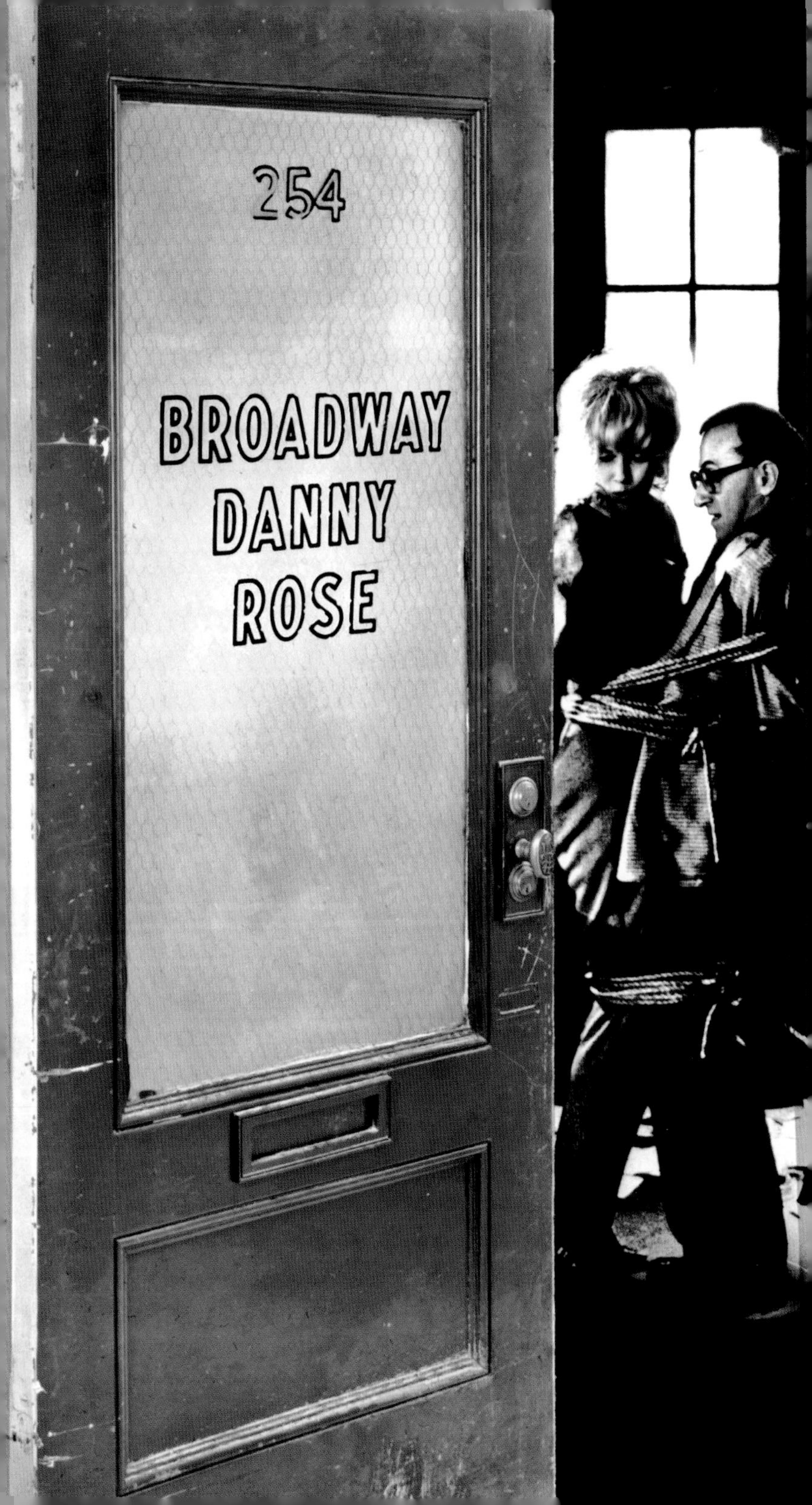
254
BROADWAY
DANNY
ROSE

Broadway Danny Rose

CERTIFICATE: **PG** | YEAR: **1984** | COUNTRY: **US** | **BW** | RUNNING TIME: **80 MINUTES**

SYNOPSIS

Danny Rose is a theatrical agent, strictly small-time, whose clients are even smaller time. The exception is an Italian crooner, Lou Canova, who is a big problem because his girlfriend Tina has a penchant for mobsters. Suddenly, Danny finds he's become the subject of a very different kind of contract.

REVIEW

Romping gleefully rather than analysing deeply, Woody Allen as director, writer and star brings his own light touch to every frame of this comedy. Putting egotistical, arty Manhattan on hold, and cutting down on his verbal wit to boot, Allen rings the changes not only by taking us to the swamps of New Jersey but also by squeezing humour primarily from situation and character rather than dialogue. He plays a small-time showbiz agent whose devotion to his one successful client knows no bounds. He'll even bring the guy's mistress to a gig while posing as her boyfriend, a set-up that her mobster ex finds most upsetting. Allen the director keeps the caper aspect on a beautifully tight leash at all times and, as the star, he sparkles with eccentricity, while Mia Farrow is amusingly, nasally blunt as a gangster's moll with daft hair. **JOHN MARRIOTT**

CAST
Woody Allen *Danny Rose* • Mia Farrow *Tina Vitale* • Nick Apollo Forte *Lou Canova* • Craig Vandenburgh *Ray Webb* • Herb Reynolds *Barney Dunn* • Paul Greco *Vito Rispoli* • Frank Renzulli *Joe Rispoli* • Edwin Bordo *Johnny Rispoli*

DIRECTOR
Woody Allen

SCREENPLAY
Woody Allen

AWARDS
Baftas (1): Original Screenplay

DVD EXTRAS
Theatrical trailer.

QUOTE UNQUOTE
I don't see you folding balloons in joints, you're gonna be folding balloons in... colleges and universities! **DANNY ROSE**

IF YOU ENJOYED THIS, WHY NOT TRY ...
Bullets over Broadway (1994)
Funny Bones (1994)

DID YOU KNOW?
Woody Allen created the role of Tina Vitale for Mia Farrow after they saw a woman with piled blonde hair and sunglasses in their favourite Italian restaurant. However, she also admits that she wore the shades because she felt her eyes weren't tough enough.

■

Carry On Cleo

CERTIFICATE: **PG** | YEAR: **1964** | COUNTRY: **UK** | **COLOUR** | RUNNING TIME: **87 MINUTES**

SYNOPSIS

Returning from a miserable campaign in Britain with not much to show for it but some puny slaves, Mark Antony is sent to Egypt to depose Cleopatra and return Ptolemy to the throne. But the Egyptian queen's charms prove persuasive and together they begin plotting against the hapless Julius Caesar.

REVIEW

Mercilessly mocking Elizabeth Taylor's disastrous *Cleopatra*, this corking ancient history lesson was filmed at Pinewood on the very same sets and sees the *Carry On* team at the peak of its powers. It's hard to know where to start lavishing the praise. The puns have never been better and the sets are positively luxuriant despite being second-hand. Amanda Barrie is exquisitely dippy in the title role, and Kenneth Connor and Jim Dale do well as the Britons in the imperial guard. But topping them all are Kenneth Williams's snivelling Caesar and Sid James's lecherous Mark Antony, whose greeting – "Tony!", "Julie!" – throughout the film is hilarious. Special mention should also go to the voice of *Gaumont British News*, EVH Emmett, who provides a wonderfully deadpan narration to the schoolboy antics.

DAVID PARKINSON

CAST

Sidney James *Mark Antony* • Kenneth Williams *Julius Caesar* • Kenneth Connor *Hengist Pod* • Charles Hawtrey *Seneca* • Joan Sims *Calpurnia* • Jim Dale *Horsa* • Amanda Barrie *Cleo* • Julie Stevens *Gloria* • Sheila Hancock *Senna Pod* • Warren Mitchell *Spencius*

DIRECTOR

Gerald Thomas

SCREENPLAY

Talbot Rothwell

DVD EXTRAS

Commentary by Amanda Barrie and Julie Stevens; photography gallery; trivia notes; theatrical trailer.

QUOTE UNQUOTE

Infamy, infamy, they've all got it in for me! JULIUS CAESAR

IF YOU ENJOYED THIS, WHY NOT TRY . . .

Cleopatra (1963)
A Funny Thing Happened on the Way to the Forum (1966)

DID YOU KNOW?

Sid James's costume was the same one worn by Richard Burton in the previous year's *Cleopatra*.

Carry On Screaming

CERTIFICATE: **PG** | YEAR: **1966** | COUNTRY: **UK** | **COLOUR** | RUNNING TIME: **92 MINUTES**

SYNOPSIS

When a young girl is abducted in a wood by a monstrous creature, Detective Sergeant Bung and Constable Slobotham are assigned to the case. Their investigation leads to the mysterious Dr Watt and his sister Valeria, who are said to be carrying out sinister experiments in their spooky mansion.

REVIEW

This is one of the finest entries in Britain's most popular comedy series. Mocking that other bastion of British cinema in the 1960s, the Hammer horror film, Talbot Rothwell's script positively bristles with classic one-liners, the most memorable being Kenneth Williams's gleeful "Frying tonight!" as he drops his victims into a bubbling cauldron of wax. In his only *Carry On*, Harry H Corbett is superb as Holmesian detective Bung, who's investigating an abduction near a spooky mansion with the help of Dr Watson-like sidekick Constable Slobotham (played by Peter Butterworth). Also impressive are Bernard Bresslaw as towering butler Sockett and Fenella Fielding as vampish vampire Valeria, but the picture belongs to Williams's undead Dr Watt, an amalgam of every mad scientist who ever set foot in a lab. **DAVID PARKINSON**

CAST

Kenneth Williams *Dr Watt* • Harry H Corbett *Detective Sergeant Bung* • Fenella Fielding *Valeria* • Jim Dale *Albert Potter* • Charles Hawtrey *Dan Dann* • Joan Sims *Emily Bung* • Bernard Bresslaw *Sockett* • Peter Butterworth *Detective Constable Slobotham* • Jon Pertwee *Dr Fettle*

DIRECTOR

Gerald Thomas

SCREENPLAY

Talbot Rothwell

DVD EXTRAS

Commentary by Angela Douglas; trivia notes; cast profiles.

QUOTE UNQUOTE

We must explore Avery Avenue! **DETECTIVE SERGEANT BUNG**

IF YOU ENJOYED THIS, WHY NOT TRY ...

Shaun of the Dead (2004)
Young Frankenstein (1974)

DID YOU KNOW?

Harry H Corbett got the role of Sidney Bung after *Carry On* stalwart Sid James pulled out through illness.

Dead Men Don't Wear Plaid

CERTIFICATE: **PG** | YEAR: **1982** | COUNTRY: **US** | **BW** | RUNNING TIME: **84 MINUTES**

SYNOPSIS

When Chandleresque private eye Rigby Reardon is hired by sultry Juliet Forrest to investigate the death of her cheese-obsessed scientist father, his search for clues leads to some very interesting characters, as stars of the *film noir* era are seamlessly inserted into the action.

REVIEW

The box-office hits came later, but Steve Martin's early collaborations with director and co-writer Carl Reiner (from *The Jerk* to *All of Me*) still rank among his best. This ingenious spoof finds Martin as a hard-boiled private eye with a dangerous phobia about cleaning women, who gets involved in a supremely silly story involving a professor and sinister Nazis. However, the story provides the slenderest of excuses for Martin to be spliced into an array of classic movies and swap dumb dialogue with stars such as Bette Davis, Burt Lancaster, Barbara Stanwyck and Ray Milland in some of their most famous roles. Martin is on inspired form and Rachel Ward is a revelation in a rare comic role. Look out, too, for Reiner himself in a cameo as Ward's butler. The antics eventually run out of steam, but along the way there are some wonderful moments for film enthusiasts. **JOHN FERGUSON**

CAST

Steve Martin *Rigby Reardon* • Rachel Ward *Juliet Forrest* • Carl Reiner *Field Marshal Von Kluck* • Reni Santoni Carlos Rodriguez • George Gaynes *Dr Forrest*

DIRECTOR

Carl Reiner

SCREENPLAY

George Gipe, Carl Reiner, Steve Martin

CONTENT ADVICE

Contains swearing.

QUOTE UNQUOTE

My plan was to kiss her with every lip on my face.
RIGBY REARDON

IF YOU ENJOYED THIS, WHY NOT TRY...

Play It Again, Sam (1972)
Zelig (1983)

DID YOU KNOW?

This proved to be the swansong of two Hollywood legends. Designer Edith Head (Oscar-nominated 34 times) not only designed the new costumes, but also those in six of the classic clips, while Miklos Rozsa's score was interwoven with themes he composed back in the 1940s and 50s.

Dr Strangelove, or How I Learned to Stop Worrying and Love the Bomb

CERTIFICATE: **PG** | YEAR: **1963** | COUNTRY: **UK** | **BW** | RUNNING TIME: **90 MINUTES**

SYNOPSIS

Believing that his impotence is the result of a Soviet plot to poison the water supply of the "free world", General Jack D Ripper dispatches nuclear-armed war planes to bomb Moscow. It is the task of President Merkin Muffley, hidden deep in the Pentagon War Room, to sort out the problem.

REVIEW

Stanley Kubrick's ferocious Cold War satire makes us smile through gritted teeth as unhinged general Sterling Hayden sends a squadron of nuclear bombers to attack Russia and trigger an apocalypse-laden doomsday machine. Peter Sellers's three performances – bemused airman, befuddled president and crazed US Nazi adviser, re-armed by the prospect of world annihilation – spiral from gentle humour to surreal horror. The scenes in which Hayden raves about "bodily fluids" and Pentagon general George C Scott rants about statistical deaths were obviously inspired by Sellers's genius. Most memorable, however, is the iconic sequence in which a B-52 pilot, Major TJ "King" Kong (Slim Pickens), straddles a nuclear bomb like a rodeo rider. Kubrick's unsparing disgust with our warlike instincts was never so obvious – or so grimly comic. **TOM HUTCHINSON**

CAST

Peter Sellers *Group Captain Lionel Mandrake/President Merkin Muffley/Dr Strangelove* • George C Scott *General "Buck" Turgidson* • Sterling Hayden *General Jack D Ripper* • Keenan Wynn *Colonel "Bat" Guano* • Slim Pickens *Major TJ "King" Kong* • Peter Bull *Ambassador de Sadesky* • Tracy Reed *Miss Scott* • James Earl Jones *Lieutenant Lothar Zogg*

DIRECTOR

Stanley Kubrick

SCREENPLAY

Stanley Kubrick, Terry Southern, Peter George, from the novel *Red Alert* by Peter George

AWARDS

Baftas (4): Film from any Source, British Film, Art Direction, UN Award

DVD EXTRAS

Collector's Edition: *Inside the Making of Dr Strangelove*; *The Art of Stanley Kubrick*; interview with Peter Sellers and George C Scott; theatrical trailer; press kit; filmographies.

CONTENT ADVICE

Contains swearing.

QUOTE UNQUOTE

Gentlemen, you can't fight in here! This is the War Room.
PRESIDENT MERKIN MUFFLEY

IF YOU ENJOYED THIS, WHY NOT TRY ...

MASH (1969)
Oh! What a Lovely War (1969)

■

DID YOU KNOW?

The aerial photograph of Burpelson Air Force Base in General Ripper's office is actually a view of Heathrow Airport.

Duck Soup

CERTIFICATE: **U** | YEAR: **1933** | COUNTRY: **US** | **BW** | RUNNING TIME: **65 MINUTES**

SYNOPSIS

Freedonia appoints a new President, Rufus T Firefly, and is soon plunged into war with neighbouring Sylvania when Firefly refuses to back down over an insult (plus he's paid a month's rent on the battlefield). Meanwhile, spies Chicolini and Pinky try to steal Freedonia's war plans.

REVIEW

The Marx Brothers reached peaks of anarchic brilliance in this comedy masterpiece, which burst upon audiences four years after their primitive feature debut in *The Cocoanuts*. Groucho, Chico, Harpo and the uncharismatic Zeppo – in his final screen role – are all entangled in a runaway satire that finds Groucho as a Ruritanian leader going to war because he has paid a month's advance rent on the battlefield. What helps make this the funniest of the Marx Brothers pictures – besides the absence of the romantic interludes that dogged later outings – are the exchanges between Groucho's Rufus T Firefly and Margaret Dumont's stately matriarch, and the zinging script ("While you're out there risking your life and limb through shot and shell, we'll be in here, thinking what a sucker you are"). If nothing else, this has to be viewed for its stunningly surreal mirror sequence. **TOM HUTCHINSON**

CAST

Groucho Marx *Rufus T Firefly* • Harpo Marx *Pinky* • Chico Marx *Chicolini* • Zeppo Marx *Bob Roland* • Margaret Dumont *Mrs Gloria Teasdale* • Raquel Torres *Vera Marcal* • Louis Calhern *Ambassador Trentino of Sylvania* • Edmund Breese *Zander* • Leonid Kinskey *Agitator* • Charles B Middleton [Charles Middleton] *Prosecutor*

DIRECTOR

Leo McCarey

SCREENPLAY

Burt Kalmar, Harry Ruby, Arthur Sheekman, Nat Perrin

QUOTE UNQUOTE

Remember, you're fighting for this woman's honour, which is probably more than she ever did. **RUFUS T FIREFLY**

IF YOU ENJOYED THIS, WHY NOT TRY . . .

Bananas (1971)
The Great Dictator (1940)

DID YOU KNOW?

The film was banned in Italy by dictator Benito Mussolini, who felt it to be a direct personal attack. The brothers were supposedly delighted by his reaction.

Female Trouble

CERTIFICATE: **18** | YEAR: **1974** | COUNTRY: **US** | **COLOUR** | RUNNING TIME: **95 MINUTES**

SYNOPSIS

Larger-than-life bad girl Dawn Davenport runs away from home when her parents fail to buy her the shoes she wanted. She gets pregnant and marries a hairdresser whose aunt wishes he were gay. But after meeting a couple who believe "crime equals beauty", Dawn's quest for notoriety truly begins.

REVIEW

Along with *Pink Flamingos*, this is the film with which cult director John Waters spectacularly redefined melodrama. A twisted parallel of *Mildred Pierce*, it features the transvestite Divine as Dawn Davenport, who embarks on a perverse quest for self-realisation following a disastrous Christmas morning in which her parents fail to deliver the requested cha-cha heels. The squeamish solo delivery of her baby is the first scene in a true mother-and-daughter-from-hell scenario, with Mink Stole in hyper tantrum mode as the insufferable brat. Their relationship only goes downhill as Dawn seeks increasingly outrageous ways to make crime pay. Also noteworthy is the overflowing, endearing Edith Massey in a category of acting all her own. Those with a sensitive disposition be warned: this is an unhinged celebration of bad taste. **DAVID OPPEDISANO**

CAST
Divine *Dawn Davenport/Earl Peterson* • David Lochary *Donald Dasher* • Mary Vivian Pearce *Donna Dasher* • Mink Stole *Taffy Davenport* • Edith Massey *Aunt Ida Nelson* • Cookie Mueller *Concetta* • Susan Walsh *Chiclet* • Michael Potter *Gater*

DIRECTOR
John Waters

SCREENPLAY
John Waters

QUOTE UNQUOTE
The world of the heterosexual is a sick and boring life.
AUNT IDA NELSON

IF YOU ENJOYED THIS, WHY NOT TRY . . .
Pink Flamingos (1972)
Women on the Verge of a Nervous Breakdown (1988)

■

DID YOU KNOW?
The film is dedicated to Manson Family member Charles "Tex" Watson.

Ferris Bueller's Day Off

CERTIFICATE: **15** | YEAR: **1986** | COUNTRY: **US** | **COLOUR** | RUNNING TIME: **98 MINUTES**

SYNOPSIS

Ferris Bueller is smart, and when he plays truant from high school he does it with style. An illicit trip to downtown Chicago involves girlfriend Sloane, best friend Cameron and a prized red Ferrari owned by Cameron's father. But with a dogged school official on his tail, Ferris's luck may be running out.

REVIEW

Matthew Broderick plays the truant of the title – worshipped by students, scourge of teachers – who whisks reluctant chum Cameron (Alan Ruck) and girlfriend Sloane (Mia Sara) off to the big city for an adventure; meanwhile, uptight dean of students Ed Rooney (Jeffrey Jones) is determined to catch him in the act. This remains the most fully rounded of late writer/director John Hughes's teen comedies, although once again it's marred slightly by Hughes's familiar undercurrent of sentimentality. Broderick is remarkably likeable as the arrogant, spoilt brat, Ruck is excellent as his melancholy friend and Jones almost steals the show as he suffers the kind of humiliations that would later be heaped upon the burglars in the Hughes-scripted blockbuster *Home Alone*. The film also provides early outings for Jennifer Grey (*Dirty Dancing*) and Charlie Sheen. **JOHN FERGUSON**

CAST

Matthew Broderick *Ferris Bueller* • Alan Ruck *Cameron Frye* • Mia Sara *Sloane Peterson* • Jeffrey Jones *Ed Rooney* • Jennifer Grey *Jeanie Bueller* • Cindy Pickett *Katie Bueller* • Lyman Ward *Tom Bueller* • Edie McClurg *School secretary* • Charlie Sheen *Garth Volbeck*

DIRECTOR

John Hughes

SCREENPLAY

John Hughes

DVD EXTRAS

Bueller... Bueller... Edition: cast featurette; making-of featurette; *Who Is Ferris Bueller?*; *The World According to Ben Stein*; *Vintage Ferris Bueller: the Lost Tapes*

QUOTE UNQUOTE

Cameron is so tight that if you stuck a lump of coal up his ass, in two weeks you'd have a diamond. **FERRIS BUELLER**

IF YOU ENJOYED THIS, WHY NOT TRY ...

Pump Up the Volume (1990)
Risky Business (1983)

DID YOU KNOW?

Because they didn't have the budget for a real Ferrari, the film-makers were forced to make three life-sized models out of fibreglass.

A Fish Called Wanda

CERTIFICATE: **15** | YEAR: **1988** | COUNTRY: **UK/US** | **COLOUR** | RUNNING TIME: **108 MINUTES**

SYNOPSIS

Respectable British barrister Archie Leach is smitten with Wanda, the flirtatious American girlfriend of the client he's defending for robbery. But what Wanda really wants is the location of the diamonds from his latest heist, as does her psychotic lover, Otto, who's waiting impatiently in the wings.

REVIEW

This hilarious tale of criminal incompetence and transatlantic eccentricity is easily John Cleese's finest achievement since *Fawlty Towers*. He excels as the uptight London barrister who becomes the dupe of scheming American thief Jamie Lee Curtis and her doltishly macho lover, Kevin Kline. But Cleese must share the credit for the film's international success with Charles Crichton, who, as the director of *The Lavender Hill Mob*, was the perfect choice for this sparkling blend of Ealing and Monty Python. Every piece of verbal or physical humour is a model of timing and restraint, whether it's Cleese's Russian-spouting striptease or the Oscar-winning Kline's merciless persecution of stuttering sidekick Michael Palin. It has an underlying darkness that recalls the work of Preston Sturges and Billy Wilder, and praise doesn't come much higher than that. **DAVID PARKINSON**

QUOTE UNQUOTE

To call you stupid would be an insult to stupid people!
WANDA

IF YOU ENJOYED THIS, WHY NOT TRY...

The Ladykillers (1955)
The Lavender Hill Mob (1951)

CAST

John Cleese *Archie Leach* • Jamie Lee Curtis *Wanda* • Kevin Kline *Otto* • Michael Palin *Ken* • Maria Aitken *Wendy* • Tom Georgeson *George* • Patricia Hayes *Mrs Coady* • Geoffrey Palmer *Judge* • Cynthia Caylor [Cynthia Cleese] *Portia*

DIRECTOR

Charles Crichton

SCREENPLAY

John Cleese, from a story by Charles Crichton, Cleese

AWARDS

Academy Awards (1): Supporting Actor (Kevin Kline)
Baftas (2): Actor (John Cleese), Supporting Actor (Kline)

DVD EXTRAS

Special Edition: commentary by John Cleese; two documentaries; two featurettes; alternative ending; deleted scenes; easter eggs; photo gallery; TV spot; theatrical trailer.

CONTENT ADVICE

Contains swearing, some violence, sex scenes, nudity.

DID YOU KNOW?

Michael Palin was criticised by some for seeming to mock people with speech impediments. In fact, Palin was drawing on personal experience – his father stuttered – and in 1993 he gave his name to the Michael Palin Centre, dedicated to helping children who stammer.

Four Weddings and a Funeral

CERTIFICATE: **15** | YEAR: **1994** | COUNTRY: **UK** | **COLOUR** | RUNNING TIME: **112 MINUTES**

SYNOPSIS

Bachelor Charles is in his 30s and a veteran of many weddings, but never as the bridegroom. Then, at a country ceremony, he meets the beautiful but elusive Carrie, who seduces him and leaves him utterly bemused when she returns to America the following day. Will he be able to forget her... ?

REVIEW

No-one could have foreseen that this glorified sitcom would change the nature of British screen comedy. The tale of a foppish bachelor (Hugh Grant), his eccentric friends and their romantic escapades is funny, charming, poignant and never anything less than hugely enjoyable. It also struck a chord with global audiences, thanks to its unique sense of understated, self-deprecating wit. Neatly structured and full of genuine warmth for its characters, Richard Curtis's Oscar-nominated screenplay is superbly observed and well served by Mike Newell's deft direction. But more important to the film's enduring appeal is the individuality of the performances. Simon Callow and the Bafta-winning Kristin Scott Thomas are outstanding alongside star Grant, who became an overnight sensation as the tousled serial ditherer haplessly pursuing his star-crossed passion for enigmatic American Andie MacDowell. **DAVID PARKINSON**

CAST

Hugh Grant *Charles* • Andie MacDowell *Carrie* • Kristin Scott Thomas *Fiona* • James Fleet *Tom* • Simon Callow *Gareth* • John Hannah *Matthew* • David Bower *David* • Charlotte Coleman *Scarlett* • Corin Redgrave *Hamish* • Rowan Atkinson *Father Gerald* • Anna Chancellor *Henrietta* • Timothy Walker *Angus* • Rosalie Crutchley *Mrs Beaumont*

DIRECTOR

Mike Newell

SCREENPLAY

Richard Curtis

AWARDS

Baftas (4): Film, Actor (Hugh Grant), Supporting Actress (Kristin Scott Thomas), Director

DVD EXTRAS

Special Edition: commentary by Mike Newell, Richard Curtis and the producers; making-of featurette; deleted scenes; a look back at the film with cast and crew; behind-the-scenes photo gallery; promotional clips; theatrical trailer.

CONTENT ADVICE

Contains swearing.

QUOTE UNQUOTE

All these weddings, all these years, all that blasted salmon and champagne. **CHARLES**

IF YOU ENJOYED THIS, WHY NOT TRY ...

Bridget Jones's Diary (2001)
Notting Hill (1999)

■

DID YOU KNOW?

It's no accident that the character played by David Hague is called Bernard, as writer Richard Curtis has always given that name to buffoonish types in his screenplays ever since Bernard Jenkin, now a tory MP, stole his girlfriend Anne.

The Full Monty

CERTIFICATE: **15** | YEAR: **1997** | COUNTRY: **UK/US** | **COLOUR** | RUNNING TIME: **87 MINUTES**

SYNOPSIS

A group of unemployed Sheffield steelworkers come up with a bold plan to restore their fortunes and capitalise on their remaining assets – taking their clothes off for money. But can they overcome their fear and embarrassment, and actually convince anyone to pay to see them do the full monty?

REVIEW

When the going gets tough, the tough get go-going, in director Peter Cattaneo's highly engaging, genuinely poignant and hilarious full-frontal comedy drama, which was nominated for 11 Baftas and won four. Robert Carlyle plays a divorced father trying to maintain joint custody of his son, who forms a strip act along with a group of other unemployed Sheffield steelworkers. Well endowed with side-splitting laughter and brilliantly performed by the superb ensemble cast, this is about men's emotional shortcomings as much as their dirty dancing techniques, and it's jam-packed with wonderful moments – the would-be Chippendales of the North absent-mindedly gyrating to the radio in a dole office is simply inspired. An Americanised musical version of the movie opened on Broadway in October 2000 and was nominated for nine Tony awards including best musical and best original score. **ALAN JONES**

CAST

Robert Carlyle *Gaz* • Tom Wilkinson *Gerald* • Mark Addy *Dave* • Lesley Sharp *Jean* • Emily Woof *Mandy* • Steve Huison *Lomper* • Paul Barber *Horse* • Hugo Speer *Guy* • Deirdre Costello *Linda* • Bruce Jones *Reg*

DIRECTOR

Peter Cattaneo

SCREENPLAY

Simon Beaufoy

AWARDS

Academy Awards (1): Original Musical or Comedy Score
Baftas (4): Film, Actor (Robert Carlyle), Supporting Actor (Tom Wilkinson), Audience Award

DVD EXTRAS

Two-disc Special Edition: two versions of the film including the American print with some of the slang taken out; commentary by Peter Cattaneo and Mark Addy; commentary from producer Umberto Pasolini; deleted scenes with optional commentary; TV ads; song highlights; development, production and aftermath featurettes; *The British Film Industry in the 90s* feature.

CONTENT ADVICE

Contains swearing, nudity.

QUOTE UNQUOTE

I've got a degree in ass-wiggling, mate. **GAZ SCHOFIELD**

IF YOU ENJOYED THIS, WHY NOT TRY ...

Brassed Off (1996)
Lucky Break (2001) ■

DID YOU KNOW?

The American distributors couldn't understand why there was no one called Monty in the film and feared this would confuse audiences. There was no confusion in China, where the Cantonese title *Six Stripped Warriors* meant *Six Naked Pigs* in Mandarin.

Galaxy Quest

CERTIFICATE: **PG** | YEAR: **1999** | COUNTRY: **US** | **COLOUR** | RUNNING TIME: **97 MINUTES**

SYNOPSIS

Almost 20 years after the cancellation of their TV show *Galaxy Quest*, the actor crew of the spaceship *Protector* encounters a strange group of fans at a convention. Believing they're being booked for a publicity gig, the actors soon realise that these are real-life aliens who need their help against a ruthless warmonger.

REVIEW

In this enormously entertaining send-up of the *Star Trek* universe, a bunch of actors from a cult sci-fi show are mistaken for the real thing and recruited to defend a threatened alien race. It's an inspired premise, fired into orbit by a fantastic script, sublime visual effects and an absolutely perfect cast. Tim Allen and Sigourney Weaver are brilliant as the show's Commander Peter Quincy Taggart and Lt Tawny Madison, but they're both upstaged by Alan Rickman as grumpy Shakespearean actor Alexander Dane, who hates his half-reptilian character Dr Lazarus. The story is so cleverly executed and the characters so beautifully fleshed-out that it not only succeeds as a *Trek* spoof, a satire on the acting profession and a parody of science-fiction fans, but also as an engaging, original space saga in its own right. **JASON CARO**

QUOTE UNQUOTE

I played Richard III. There were five curtain calls. I was an actor once, damn it. Now look at me. Look at me! I won't go out there and say that stupid line one more time.
ALEXANDER DANE

IF YOU ENJOYED THIS, WHY NOT TRY . . .

Free Enterprise (1998)
Trekkies (1997)

CAST

Tim Allen *Jason Nesmith/Commander Peter Quincy Taggart* • Sigourney Weaver *Gwen DeMarco/Lt Tawny Madison* • Alan Rickman *Alexander Dane/Dr Lazarus* • Tony Shalhoub *Fred Kwan/Tech Sgt Chen* • Sam Rockwell *Guy Fleegman* • Daryl Mitchell *Tommy Webber/Laredo* • Enrico Colantoni *Mathesar* • Robin Sachs *Sarris* • Patrick Breen *Quellek*

DIRECTOR

Dean Parisot

SCREENPLAY

Robert Gordon, David Howard, from a story by Howard

DVD EXTRAS

On Location in Space feature; deleted scenes; production notes and filmmakers' biographies; Thermian language audio track; theatrical trailers.

DID YOU KNOW?

The idea for the movie came to co-writer David Howard when he heard a Leonard Nimoy voiceover on an Imax trailer.

The General

CERTIFICATE: **U** | YEAR: **1927** | COUNTRY: **US** | **BW** | RUNNING TIME: **73 MINUTES**

SYNOPSIS

At the onset of the American Civil War, a humble railroad engineer tries to enlist in the Confederate Army but is rejected. His sweetheart wrongly thinks that he won't join up because he's a coward. Then his train – with his girl on board – is stolen by Union agents, and the engineer finds himself risking all in pursuit.

REVIEW

Buster Keaton's greatest movie is, some would argue, the finest silent screen comedy ever made. Playing Johnnie Gray, the stone-faced engineer who loves his vast steam locomotive, "The General", almost as much as his girlfriend, Keaton shows his genius in the creation of an endearing character over and above the nuts and bolts of comic invention. Keaton's narrow range of emotion becomes a positive boon, making Johnnie a hapless plaything of fate, and his efforts to rescue his stolen train and impress his girl almost heroic. And, when combined with the imaginative, athletic and downright dangerous stunts that Keaton pulls off in the process, the movie becomes an adventure to rival any of today's computer-enhanced efforts. The humour ranges from the gentle to the exhilarating, while the drama of the railroad chase has a visual beauty that puts this comedy into the category of true classic. **TOM HUTCHINSON**

CAST

Buster Keaton *Johnnie Gray* • Marion Mack *Annabelle Lee* • Charles Smith *Her father* • Frank Barnes *Her brother* • Glen Cavender *Capt Anderson, chief spy* • Jim Farley [James Farley] *Gen Thatcher* • Frank Hagney *Recruiting officer* • Frederick Vroom *Confederate general*

DIRECTOR

Buster Keaton, Clyde Bruckman

SCREENPLAY

Buster Keaton, Clyde Bruckman, Al Boasberg, Charles Smith, from the novel *The Great Locomotive Chase* by William Pittinger

DVD EXTRAS

Special Edition: introduction by David Robinson; restoration featurette; recording the new score featurette; documentary on Buster Keaton; extract from the tinted version of the film; three short films including *The Railroader*, sequel to *The General*; two other featurettes, one featuring Orson Welles on the film.

QUOTE UNQUOTE

There were two loves in his life: his engine and... [Johnnie is holding a picture of Annabelle] **INTERTITLE**

IF YOU ENJOYED THIS, WHY NOT TRY ...

Go West (1940)
Safety Last (1923)

DID YOU KNOW?

When the steam engine The Texas plunged off the collapsing bridge, it was the most expensive single shot filmed during the silent era. Six cameras were used to capture the stunt, which cost $42,000 (the equivalent of some $2 million today).

Gentlemen Prefer Blondes

CERTIFICATE: **U** | YEAR: **1953** | COUNTRY: **US** | **COLOUR** | RUNNING TIME: **87 MINUTES**

SYNOPSIS

Showgirls Lorelei Lee and Dorothy Shaw sail for Paris when Lorelei's millionaire fiancé fails to make the trip. Lorelei proclaims her mission to find Dorothy a husband, but is distracted by an elderly gent's diamond mine, while Dorothy falls for a private eye who's spying on Lorelei.

REVIEW

Marilyn Monroe's star was well and truly rising when she portrayed author Anita Loos's gold-digging Lorelei Lee in this scintillating 20th Century-Fox musical. It's cannily directed by Howard Hawks, who had a clever understanding of how to exploit Monroe's star power – he'd previously directed her in *Monkey Business*. Watch how even co-star Jane Russell is entranced by the blonde bombshell during their duets. Monroe shines in the brilliantly choreographed production numbers, most notably *Diamonds Are a Girl's Best Friend* (and if you can take your eyes off her, you can look out for a young George Chakiris from the *West Side Story* cast in the chorus). The third act is a contrived letdown but, make no mistake, this is the movie that consolidated Monroe's stardom and showcased her special talent to the full.
TONY SLOMAN

CAST

Marilyn Monroe *Lorelei Lee* • Jane Russell *Dorothy Shaw* • Charles Coburn *Sir Francis Beekman* • Elliott Reid *Malone* • Tommy Noonan *Gus Esmond* • George Winslow *Henry Spofford III* • Taylor Holmes *Gus Esmond Sr*

DIRECTOR

Howard Hawks

SCREENPLAY

Charles Lederer, from the play by Anita Loos, Joseph Fields, from the novel by Anita Loos

QUOTE UNQUOTE

I always say a kiss on the hand might feel very good, but a diamond tiara lasts forever. **LORELEI LEE**

IF YOU ENJOYED THIS, WHY NOT TRY . . .

How to Marry a Millionaire (1953)
Three Coins in the Fountain (1954)

DID YOU KNOW?

The ship model and some of the internal ocean liner sets employed here were originally used in 1953's *Titanic* starring Clifton Webb and Barbara Stanwyck.

Ghost Busters

CERTIFICATE: **PG** | YEAR: **1984** | COUNTRY: **US** | **COLOUR** | RUNNING TIME: **105 MINUTES**

SYNOPSIS

Three New York university professors researching parapsychology set up in business for themselves when their grant is withdrawn. Clients prove to be thin on the ground at first, but the "ghost busters" are soon in demand when a spook invasion threatens to turn New York City upside down.

REVIEW

The special effects-driven slapstick tends to overshadow the fact that there are some slyer, more sophisticated laughs on offer in this blockbusting family comedy. Bill Murray is terrifically deadpan and sleazy as the dubious leader of a company of ghost busters (also including the film's co-writers Dan Aykroyd and Harold Ramis, plus Ernie Hudson), who are called into action when ancient spirits are let loose in New York. Sigourney Weaver shows an admirably light touch as the possessed cellist who Murray takes more than just a professional interest in, and Rick Moranis's turn as her geeky neighbour proved to be his breakthrough role. Director Ivan Reitman stages some spectacular set pieces, culminating in an enjoyably daft finale featuring a giant marshmallow man. The concept was so successful that it spawned a cartoon series, and almost the entire team reunited for the 1989 sequel. **JOHN FERGUSON**

QUOTE UNQUOTE

I make it a rule never to get involved with possessed people. **DR PETER VENKMAN**

IF YOU ENJOYED THIS, WHY NOT TRY ...

Evolution (2001)
Men in Black (1997)

■

CAST

Bill Murray *Dr Peter Venkman* • Dan Aykroyd *Dr Raymond Stantz* • Sigourney Weaver *Dana Barrett* • Harold Ramis *Dr Egon Spengler* • Rick Moranis *Louis Tully* • Annie Potts *Janine Melnitz* • Ernie Hudson *Winston Zeddemore* • William Atherton *Walter Peck*

DIRECTOR

Ivan Reitman

SCREENPLAY

Dan Aykroyd, Harold Ramis

AWARDS

Baftas (1): Original Song (*Ghost Busters*)

DVD EXTRAS

Commentary by Ivan Reitman, Harold Ramis and Joe Medjuck; deleted scenes; storyboard to film comparison; meeting the special effects crew; behind-the-scenes featurette; conceptual artwork; photo gallery; theatrical trailer; *Ghostbusters 2* trailer. Also available on Blu-ray.

DID YOU KNOW?

The part of Peter Venkman was originally written for John Belushi by Dan Aykroyd, but Belushi died of a drugs overdose before the screenplay was finished, so Bill Murray got the role instead.

The Graduate

CERTIFICATE: **15** | YEAR: **1967** | COUNTRY: **US** | **COLOUR** | RUNNING TIME: **101 MINUTES**

SYNOPSIS

Recent college graduate Benjamin Braddock returns home to discover a new "tutor" in the form of a friend of his parents. Benjamin seems adrift in his own life, so the alcoholic Mrs Robinson decides that what he needs is instruction in more physical matters after his intellectual struggles.

REVIEW

This landmark satire on America's bourgeoisie thrust the unknown Dustin Hoffman into the limelight and won a best director Oscar for Mike Nichols. In his first major role, Hoffman is sensational as the innocent college graduate who is seduced by older married woman Anne Bancroft and then falls for her daughter Katharine Ross. The humour in Calder Willingham and Buck Henry's screenplay has the bite of a dry martini, Robert Surtees's stunning, innovative camerawork contributes telling visual ironies (especially in the scene where Hoffman runs to the church) and the Simon and Garfunkel soundtrack perfectly captures the mood of disaffected youth seething beneath the laid-back exterior of 1960s California. Nichols's Oscar was well deserved, and launched him into the top rank of Hollywood directors, while his three leads were also nominated but failed to win. **TOM HUTCHINSON**

CAST

Dustin Hoffman *Benjamin Braddock* • Anne Bancroft *Mrs Robinson* • Katharine Ross *Elaine Robinson* • William Daniels *Mr Braddock* • Elizabeth Wilson *Mrs Braddock* • Murray Hamilton *Mr Robinson* • Brian Avery *Carl Smith* • Walter Brooke *Mr Maguire*

DIRECTOR

Mike Nichols

SCREENPLAY

Calder Willingham, Buck Henry, from the novel by Charles Webb

AWARDS

Academy Awards (1): Director
Baftas (5): Film, Most Promising Newcomer (Dustin Hoffman), Director, Screenplay, Editing

DVD EXTRAS

Collector's Edition: *The Graduate at 25* documentary; original widescreen excerpts; interview with Dustin Hoffman.

CONTENT ADVICE

Contains sex scenes, nudity.

QUOTE UNQUOTE

Mrs Robinson, you're trying to seduce me. Aren't you?
BENJAMIN BRADDOCK

IF YOU ENJOYED THIS, WHY NOT TRY . . .

Goodbye, Columbus (1969)
Harold and Maude (1972) ■

DID YOU KNOW?

Although it is Dustin Hoffman on the original poster, he's not staring at Anne Bancroft's leg. The limb in question belonged to a pre-*Dallas* Linda Gray, who went on to play Mrs Robinson in 2001 in London's West End, revealing a good deal more than a bit of leg.

The Great Dictator

CERTIFICATE: **U** | YEAR: **1940** | COUNTRY: **US** | **BW** | RUNNING TIME: **124 MINUTES**

SYNOPSIS

A Jewish barber in a Tomanian ghetto wakes from years of amnesia to find himself a subject of an ominous dictator called Adenoid Hynkel, to whom he bears a startling resemblance. As storm troopers daub his shop window, he finds help from Hannah, a downtrodden laundress who also lives in the ghetto.

REVIEW

Hitler didn't see the joke, but he got the point – Charlie Chaplin's first dialogue feature (made 12 years after the introduction of sound) was a satire on the anti-Semitic Nazi regime. In a variation on his Little Tramp persona (with the toothbrush moustache drawing an obvious comparison to Hitler), Chaplin plays the dual role of a Jewish barber and dictator Adenoid Hynkel. The final speech, pleading for universal tolerance, is mawkish outrage. Before that, however, we have the glories of the barber shaving a customer in time to a Hungarian dance by Brahms contrasting with Hynkel's solo ballet with a globe. Bliss, even though Chaplin said that, if he'd known of the Nazis' real horror, he would never have made such a burlesque. This was the first time audiences had heard the Little Tramp speak, and it was also the last as Chaplin never played the little man with the moustache again. **TOM HUTCHINSON**

QUOTE UNQUOTE

How wonderful! Tomania, a nation of blue-eyed blonds.
ADENOID HYNKEL

IF YOU ENJOYED THIS, WHY NOT TRY ...

Dad's Army (1971)
Inglourious Basterds (2009)
To Be or Not to Be (1942)

CAST

Charles Chaplin *Jewish barber/Hynkel, dictator of Tomania* • Paulette Goddard *Hannah* • Jack Oakie *Napaloni, dictator of Bacteria* • Reginald Gardiner *Schultz* • Henry Daniell *Garbitsch* • Billy Gilbert *Herring* • Grace Hayle *Madame Napaloni* • Carter DeHaven *Bacterian ambassador*

DIRECTOR

Charles Chaplin

SCREENPLAY

Charles Chaplin

DVD EXTRAS

The Chaplin Collection version: *The Tramp and the Dictator* - documentary by Kevin Brownlow and Michael Kloft; colour footage shot on set by Sydney Chaplin; compilation of scenes from other Chaplin films; deleted scene from *Charlie the Barber* shot in 1919.

DID YOU KNOW?

Although the Führer banned the film throughout occupied Europe, he reportedly secured his own copy and watched it twice. Chaplin later remarked, "I'd give anything to know what he thought of it."

Grosse Pointe Blank

CERTIFICATE: **15** | YEAR: **1997** | COUNTRY: **US** | **COLOUR** | RUNNING TIME: **102 MINUTES**

SYNOPSIS

Professional hitman Martin Blank has issues. A job has gone wrong, he's obsessed with an old flame and his high-school reunion is looming. Advised by his exasperated and rather fearful therapist to get out of town, Blank heads for Grosse Pointe to catch up, kick back and maybe fit in an assassination.

REVIEW

Named in tribute to John Boorman's cult thriller *Point Blank*, this inventive black comedy drama stars John Cusack as hitman Martin Blank, who returns to his home town of Grosse Pointe (a suburb of Detroit) for a high-school reunion and another assassination. He bumps into the old flame (Minnie Driver) he jilted on prom night ten years before and discovers that conventional free-marketeers are just as ruthless as he is. Director George Armitage keeps the action smart and edgy (Cusack's real-life kickboxing instructor is highly effective as his would-be assassin), and there are some fine performances from a supporting cast that includes Dan Aykroyd (as a pushy fellow hitman), Alan Arkin (as Blank's reluctant shrink) and Joan Cusack. And if you're a *Dharma & Greg* fan, this marked Jenna Elfman's big-screen debut. **TOM HUTCHINSON**

QUOTE UNQUOTE

Hi! I'm Martin Blank, do you remember me? I'm not married, I don't have any kids, and I'd blow your head off if someone paid me enough. **MARTIN Q BLANK**

IF YOU ENJOYED THIS, WHY NOT TRY...

Mr & Mrs Smith (2005)
Prizzi's Honor (1985)

CAST

John Cusack *Martin Q Blank* • Minnie Driver *Debi Newberry* • Alan Arkin *Dr Oatman* • Dan Aykroyd *Mr Grocer* • Joan Cusack *Marcella* • Hank Azaria *Lardner* • K Todd Freeman *McCullers* • Mitchell Ryan *Mr Newberry*

DIRECTOR

George Armitage

SCREENPLAY

Tom Jankiewicz, DV DeVincentis, Steve Pink, John Cusack, from a story by Jankiewicz

CONTENT ADVICE

Contains swearing, violence.

DID YOU KNOW?

Actors John and Joan Cusack are joined here by two of their lesser-known siblings – sister Ann and brother Bill.

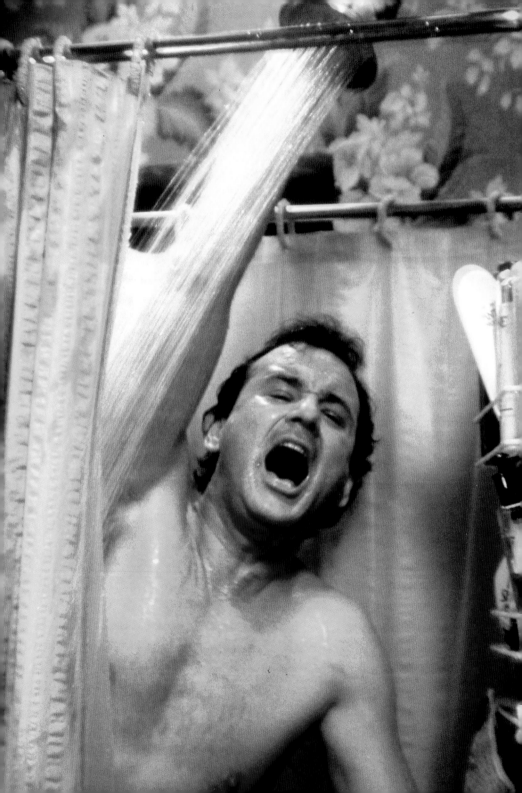

Groundhog Day

CERTIFICATE: **PG** | YEAR: **1993** | COUNTRY: **US** | **COLOUR** | RUNNING TIME: **96 MINUTES**

SYNOPSIS

A cynical TV weatherman is sent to cover the annual Groundhog Day festival in Pennsylvania. Stranded by a snowstorm, he wakes the following morning to discover that the previous day is repeating itself – but only for him. Is he doomed to live the same day for ever, or can he escape the time trap?

REVIEW

Director Harold Ramis's hilariously repetitive movie is a strong contender for best comedy of the 1990s. Bill Murray gives one of the best performances of his career as Phil Connors, the weatherman with attitude, trapped in a day he will remember for the rest of his life because, unless he can find some answers, it will *be* the rest of his life. Stephen Tobolowsky is superb as a nerdy insurance salesman and, as Murray's TV producer, Andie MacDowell has never been better. Ramis uses every cinematic trick in the book to keep what is essentially a one-gag movie brimming with life and fresh ideas, and Murray brings on his character's gradual redemption without breaking his comic stride. It is said that the pair argued over the balance of the philosophical and comic in the movie, and it is just that mix of thoughtful and funny that elevates *Groundhog Day* above its peers. **DAVID PARKINSON**

QUOTE UNQUOTE

Well, what if there is no tomorrow? There wasn't one today. **PHIL CONNORS**

IF YOU ENJOYED THIS, WHY NOT TRY . . .

The Truman Show (1998)
12:01 (1993)

CAST

Bill Murray *Phil Connors* • Andie MacDowell *Rita Hanson* • Chris Elliott *Larry* • Stephen Tobolowsky *Ned* • Brian Doyle-Murray *Buster* • Marita Geraghty *Nancy* • Angela Paton *Mrs Lancaster* • Rick Ducommun *Gus*

DIRECTOR

Harold Ramis

SCREENPLAY

Danny Rubin, Harold Ramis, from a story by Rubin

AWARDS

Baftas (1): Original Screenplay

DVD EXTRAS

Collector's Edition: commentary by Harold Ramis; documentary *The Weight of Time*; filmographies of Harold Ramis, Bill Murray, Andie MacDowell, Chris Elliott.

CONTENT ADVICE

Contains swearing.

DID YOU KNOW?

Director Harold Ramis has said that Phil repeats Groundhog Day for ten years until he breaks the cycle, which would be 3,650-odd days. The movie only shows one per cent of those days – around 37 in all.

Harold and Maude

CERTIFICATE: **15** | YEAR: **1972** | COUNTRY: **US** | **COLOUR** | RUNNING TIME: **87 MINUTES**

SYNOPSIS

Harold Chasen, the quiet son of a domineering mother, has no friends and but a single interest – a calm fascination with death. Then, on one of his regular visits to a stranger's funeral, he meets a fellow enthusiast, a feisty elderly lady called Maude, and a most unusual relationship blossoms.

REVIEW

Depressed by life, and rejected by his wealthy mother (Vivian Pickles), teenager Harold (Bud Cort) is fascinated by death, drives a hearse and gatecrashes funerals for fun. It's at a graveyard that he meets 79-year-old free spirit Maude (Ruth Gordon), and the pair then embark on an unlikely relationship. You could call it bad taste, but rarely has such a strange love affair been presented so charmingly as in this cult classic from director Hal Ashby (*Being There*). The performances of the wonderfully poker-faced Cort and the irrepressible Gordon make the central premise – that love can blossom at any age – believable and moving, in a movie that, for all its eccentricities, likes people. As screenwriter Colin Higgins said, "We're all Harold, and we all want to be Maude. We're all repressed and trying to be free". Cat Stevens's soundtrack is an added delight.

TOM HUTCHINSON

CAST

Ruth Gordon *Maude* • Bud Cort *Harold* • Vivian Pickles *Mrs Chasen* • Cyril Cusack *Glaucus* • Charles Tyner *Uncle Victor* • Ellen Geer *Sunshine Dore* • Eric Christmas *Priest* • G Wood *Psychiatrist*

DIRECTOR

Hal Ashby

SCREENPLAY

Colin Higgins

DVD EXTRAS

Theatrical trailer.

QUOTE UNQUOTE

Everyone has the right to make an ass out of themselves. You just can't let the world judge you too much. **MAUDE**

IF YOU ENJOYED THIS, WHY NOT TRY ...

The Loved One (1965)
Rushmore (1998)

DID YOU KNOW?

Bud Cort's career stalled after making the film and he has said "I've had my moments where I just cursed that movie and wished I'd never done it."

Harvey

CERTIFICATE: **U** | YEAR: **1950** | COUNTRY: **US** | **BW** | RUNNING TIME: **107 MINUTES**

SYNOPSIS

Tippler Elwood P Dowd has a constant companion, Harvey, a six-foot white rabbit who just happens to be invisible to everyone else. Elwood is content but his loyalty to Harvey is enough to wreck the life and hopes of his socially prominent sister and spinster niece, and drastic action is called for.

REVIEW

James Stewart gives a knockout performance in this classic comic fantasy (from Mary Chase's 1944 Pulitzer Prize-winning Broadway play) about tipsy Elwood P Dowd and his unusual friendship with Harvey, an invisible six-foot-tall white rabbit. This is superb whimsy about the fine line between sanity and insanity, and director Henry Koster handles this loving tribute to eccentricity and bar-room philosophy with a deft touch. Alongside the satiric misunderstandings, character mix-ups and revitalised clichés come poignant comments about humanity's lack of communication, which touch both the funny bone and the heart. It's guaranteed to leave you with a smile on your face for ages afterwards. Koster would go on to direct Stewart in four further films, and would probably turn in his grave if he knew that Steven Spielberg is rumoured to be working on a *Harvey* remake. **ALAN JONES**

CAST

James Stewart *Elwood P Dowd* • Josephine Hull *Veta Louise Simmons* • Peggy Dow *Miss Kelly* • Charles Drake *Dr Sanderson* • Cecil Kellaway *Dr Chumley* • Victoria Horne *Myrtle Mae* • Jesse White *Wilson* • William Lynn *Judge Gaffney* • Wallace Ford *Lofgren*

DIRECTOR

Henry Koster

SCREENPLAY

Mary Chase, Oscar Brodney, from the play by Chase

AWARDS

Academy Awards (1): Supporting Actress (Josephine Hull)

DVD EXTRAS

Special introduction by James Stewart; theatrical trailer; production notes; cast and crew biographies; film highlights.

QUOTE UNQUOTE

Well, I've wrestled with reality for 35 years, doctor, and I'm happy to state I finally won out over it. **ELWOOD P DOWD**

IF YOU ENJOYED THIS, WHY NOT TRY...

It's a Wonderful Life (1946)
Miracle on 34th Street (1947)

DID YOU KNOW?

James Stewart's portrayal of Elwood P Dowd was to be a part of his life for three decades. Having featured in the original Broadway production and this screen remake, he went on to star again in the 1970 Broadway revival and the 1972 TV movie remake.

Heathers

CERTIFICATE: **18** | YEAR: **1989** | COUNTRY: **US** | **COLOUR** | RUNNING TIME: **98 MINUTES**

SYNOPSIS

Veronica Sawyer's desire for high-school popularity draws her into a clique of students led by three domineering girls, all named Heather. As Veronica grows resentful of the trio's behaviour, she becomes involved with rebel loner Jason Dean and they plan revenge – but one of them isn't playing.

REVIEW

Don't let the fact that Michael Lehmann went on to direct the flop Bruce Willis caper movie *Hudson Hawk* put you off his stunning debut – a prime cult movie about an all-girl high-school clique that terrorises fellow students. Their actions prompt cool couple Winona Ryder and Christian Slater (firing on all cylinders like a young Jack Nicholson) to engineer a rash of deaths to break the clique's hold on their schoolmates – deemed by them a clueless bunch of college "Swatch Dogs" and "Diet Coke Heads". Beneath the hip, lip-glossed surface of this devastatingly witty black comedy lurks a serious satire on peer-group pretensions and other teen movies. But the message never gets in the way of the snappy dialogue or on-target jabs at the in-crowd lunacy of high-school life. **ALAN JONES**

QUOTE UNQUOTE

If you were happy every day of your life, you wouldn't be a human being. You'd be a game-show host. **VERONICA SAWYER**

IF YOU ENJOYED THIS, WHY NOT TRY ...

Election (1999)
Mean Girls (2004)

CAST

Winona Ryder *Veronica Sawyer* • Christian Slater *Jason "JD" Dean* • Shannen Doherty *Heather Duke* • Lisanne Falk *Heather McNamara* • Kim Walker *Heather Chandler* • Penelope Milford *Pauline Fleming* • Glenn Shadix *Father Ripper* • Lance Fenton *Kurt Kelly* • Patrick Labyorteaux *Ram Sweeney*

DIRECTOR

Michael Lehmann

SCREENPLAY

Daniel Waters

DVD EXTRAS

Commentary by director Michael Lehmann, producer Denise Di Novi and writer Daniel Waters; *Swatch Dogs and Diet Coke Heads* documentary; theatrical trailer; excerpt from screenplay with original ending; talent biographies.

CONTENT ADVICE

Contains violence, swearing, sex scenes.

DID YOU KNOW?

The producers originally wanted to use *The Catcher in the Rye* as the book that suicidal students referred to in the movie, but were unable to get permission. *Moby Dick* was therefore used instead.

■

John Cusack   High Fidelity

High Fidelity

CERTIFICATE: **15** | YEAR: **2000** | COUNTRY: **US/UK** | **COLOUR** | RUNNING TIME: **108 MINUTES**

SYNOPSIS

Rob, the owner of a hip if under-frequented Chicago record store, has just broken up with his girlfriend and is struggling to make sense of his life. With the help of his two co-workers, his beloved music and his top-five list of failed relationships, he sets out on a voyage of self-discovery.

REVIEW

Don't fret about the fact that Stephen Frears has transposed Nick Hornby's novel from north London to downtown Chicago. This slickly scripted, knowingly played and cameo-strewn comedy stands on its merits as an *Alfie* for the millennial generation. As the owner of a failing vinyl emporium, John Cusack combines reluctant self-awareness with genuine delusion as he attempts to reconcile the loss of girlfriend Iben Hjejle to lusty neighbour Tim Robbins (this is one of six films Cusack has made with Robbins – the first was 1985's *The Sure Thing*) by dating singer Lisa Bonet. However, it's when directly addressing the viewer or compulsively compiling "top five" lists with co-workers Jack Black (in his breakthrough role) and Todd Louiso that Cusack, and the picture, really come alive. **DAVID PARKINSON**

CAST
John Cusack *Rob Gordon* • Iben Hjejle *Laura* • Todd Louiso *Dick* • Jack Black *Barry* • Lisa Bonet *Marie De Salle* • Catherine Zeta-Jones *Charlie* • Joan Cusack *Liz* • Tim Robbins *Ian* • Lili Taylor *Sarah* • Natasha Gregson Wagner *Caroline*

DIRECTOR
Stephen Frears

SCREENPLAY
DV DeVincentis, Steve Pink, John Cusack, Scott Rosenberg, from the novel by Nick Hornby

DVD EXTRAS
Deleted scenes; interview with Stephen Frears; interview with John Cusack; theatrical trailer.

CONTENT ADVICE
Contains swearing, a sex scene, brief nudity.

QUOTE UNQUOTE
Do I listen to pop music because I'm miserable? Or am I miserable because I listen to pop music? **ROB GORDON**

IF YOU ENJOYED THIS, WHY NOT TRY . . .
Fever Pitch (1996)
The School of Rock (2003)

DID YOU KNOW?
The book was also adapted into a Broadway stage musical, which ran for only 11 days at the Imperial Theater in December 2006.

His Girl Friday

CERTIFICATE: **U** | YEAR: **1939** | COUNTRY: **US** | **BW** | RUNNING TIME: **91 MINUTES**

SYNOPSIS

When fast-talking newspaper editor Walter Burns discovers that his star reporter Hildy Johnson, who just happens to be his ex-wife, is planning to quit her job for a life of domestic bliss, he sets about trying to win her back with a juicy story. But is it just her reporting skills he's going to miss?

REVIEW

This brilliant reworking of the classic newspaper play *The Front Page* from director Howard Hawks is the fastest-talking comedy in the history of Hollywood, and the perfect vehicle for Cary Grant (never better) and Grant's then girlfriend, Rosalind Russell (never tougher). Limited for most of the time to two sets (the newspaper office and the pressroom at the jail), the film's great strength is the interplay between the two leads, who star as former spouses having a tough time remaining apart. It also boasts one of the blackest comedy situations ever, as a small-time loser finds himself up against city corruption and imminent execution. Clever, witty and extremely satisfying, this marvellous film is still achingly funny today and was never bettered, despite two further remakes, in 1974 (Billy Wilder's *The Front Page*) and in 1988 (*Switching Channels*, with Burt Reynolds). **TONY SLOMAN**

QUOTE UNQUOTE

I wish you hadn't done that, Hildy ...divorce me. Makes a fellow lose all faith in himself... Almost gives him a feeling he wasn't wanted. **WALTER BURNS**

IF YOU ENJOYED THIS, WHY NOT TRY ...

The Front Page (1931)
The Front Page (1974)

CAST

Cary Grant *Walter Burns* • Rosalind Russell *Hildy Johnson* • Ralph Bellamy *Bruce Baldwin* • Gene Lockhart *Sheriff Peter B Hartwell* • Porter Hall *Murphy* • Ernest Truex *Roy B Bensinger* • Cliff Edwards *Endicott* • Clarence Kolb *Mayor* • Billy Gilbert *Joe Pettibone*

DIRECTOR

Howard Hawks

SCREENPLAY

Charles Lederer, from the play *The Front Page* by Ben Hecht, Charles MacArthur

DVD EXTRAS

Columbia Classics edition: Cary Grant *Making Headlines* featurette; Howard Hawks *Reporter's Notebook* featurette; Rosalind Russell *The Inside Scoop* featurette; commentary by film critic and author Todd McCarthy; vintage advertising photo gallery; theatrical trailer; filmographies.

DID YOU KNOW?

Howard Hawks originally planned a straight remake of newspaper comedy *The Front Page* with two male leads. However, he so liked the way that his secretary read Hildy's lines while auditioning some supporting roles that he decided to cast an actress.

Horse Feathers

CERTIFICATE: **U** | YEAR: **1932** | COUNTRY: **US** | **BW** | RUNNING TIME: **63 MINUTES**

SYNOPSIS

John Quincy Adams Wagstaff is the new and not entirely competent President of Huxley College, where American football is king. He learns that rivals Darwin University have acquired professional players, but an attempt to improve his own team leads to mayhem as an inept bootlegger and a dogcatcher sign on.

REVIEW

In their penultimate movie for Paramount Pictures, Groucho, Chico, Harpo and, this time around, Zeppo, display a wonderful disarray of puns, slapstick and misunderstandings, as Groucho becomes head of Huxley College just as it needs to win a crucial Thanksgiving Day American football game. In fact, he's taken the job to save his student son (Zeppo), who's been at the college for 12 years, from a life of debauchery ("I came into this college to get my son out of it"). Chico, in the meantime, operates out of a speakeasy and is mistaken along with dogcatcher Harpo for the famous football players Groucho needs to win the game. This timeless and unmissable classic was followed by the even more anarchic *Duck Soup*, before the brothers decamped to MGM, where their inspired chaotic style was sadly eventually reined in. **TOM HUTCHINSON**

QUOTE UNQUOTE

As I look out among your smiling, eager faces, I can readily understand why this college is flat on its back.
PROFESSOR WAGSTAFF

IF YOU ENJOYED THIS, WHY NOT TRY . . .

College (1927)
The Freshman (1925)

CAST

Groucho Marx *Professor Wagstaff* • Harpo Marx *Pinky* • Chico Marx *Baravelli* • Zeppo Marx *Frank* • Thelma Todd *Connie Bailey* • David Landau *Jennings* • James Pierce *Mullens* • Nat Pendleton *McCarthy*

DIRECTOR

Norman Z McLeod

SCREENPLAY

Bert Kalmar, Harry Ruby, SJ Perelman, Will B Johnstone, with additional dialogue by Arthur Sheekman

DID YOU KNOW?

Woody Allen took inspiration for the title of his 1996 musical comedy *Everyone Says I Love You* from this film's satirical romantic ballad of the same name.

I'm All Right Jack

CERTIFICATE: **U** | YEAR: **1959** | COUNTRY: **UK** | **BW** | RUNNING TIME: **100 MINUTES**

SYNOPSIS

After failing to find a position in management, naive Oxford graduate Stanley Windrush takes a job on the shop floor of his conniving uncle's armaments factory. When he admits to not being in the union, by-the-book shop steward Fred Kite suspects he's a time-and-motion man and demands his dismissal.

REVIEW

The Boulting Brothers' sparkling comedy of industrial manners places the principal characters from their 1956 national service classic *Private's Progress* in civvy street as they embark on postwar careers. The scene this time is a factory where Dennis Price and Richard Attenborough are once more knee-deep in shady dealings, and in need of naive Oxford graduate Ian Carmichael to unwittingly carry them through. Terry-Thomas also returns from the earlier film, now the personnel manager driven to distraction by Carmichael's incompetence. But stealing the entire show is Peter Sellers as Fred Kite, the union official chained to the rule book, whose faith in communism is inspired by thoughts of "all them cornfields and ballet in the evenings". Although the film lampoons workers and management alike, it seems like an ardent attack on the unions, purely because Sellers's performance is so astonishing. **DAVID PARKINSON**

QUOTE UNQUOTE

We do not and cannot accept the principle that incompetence justifies dismissal. That is victimisation.
FRED KITE

IF YOU ENJOYED THIS, WHY NOT TRY . . .

The Man in the White Suit (1951)
Private's Progress (1956)

CAST
Ian Carmichael *Stanley Windrush* • Peter Sellers *Fred Kite* • Terry-Thomas *Major Hitchcock* • Richard Attenborough *Sidney de Vere Cox* • Dennis Price *Bertram Tracepurcel* • Margaret Rutherford *Aunt Dolly* • Irene Handl *Mrs Kite* • Liz Fraser *Cynthia Kite* • John Le Mesurier *Waters*

DIRECTOR
John Boulting

SCREENPLAY
Frank Harvey, Alan Hackney, John Boulting, from the novel *Private Life* by Hackney

AWARDS
Baftas (2): British Actor (Peter Sellers), Screenplay

DID YOU KNOW?
Such was the perceived power of this trade union comedy that the BBC cancelled a transmission planned for the day before the 1979 General Election, in case it swayed voters' opinions.

It Happened One Night

CERTIFICATE: **U** | YEAR: **1934** | COUNTRY: **US** | **BW** | RUNNING TIME: **100 MINUTES**

SYNOPSIS

A hard-nosed reporter stumbles across the scoop of a lifetime when he meets up with a wealthy heiress on the run from her father. He agrees to help her reach her fiancé in return for the exclusive story, but as mishap follows misfortune, the thrown-together pair begin to fall for each other.

REVIEW

This started out as a minor film called "Night Bus" and then MGM decided to punish its errant star Clark Gable by sending him over to Columbia to play the reporter. And what happened? As classy and charming a romantic comedy as you're ever likely to see, winning Oscars in all key departments – best film, director, stars, screenplay (only *One Flew over the Cuckoo's Nest* and *The Silence of the Lambs* have matched that achievement) – thanks to whizzkid director Frank Capra and a marvellous foil to Gable in leading lady Claudette Colbert. The scene where runaway heiress Colbert hitches a lift and the infamous "Walls of Jericho" bedroom sequence have great charm, and confirm this stand-out movie's claim to classic status. Incidentally, Gable changed American fashion overnight in the bit where he strips off his shirt and reveals that he's not wearing a vest! **TONY SLOMAN**

CAST

Clark Gable *Peter Warne* • Claudette Colbert *Ellie Andrews* • Walter Connolly *Alexander Andrews* • Roscoe Karns *Oscar Shapeley* • Jameson Thomas *King Westley* • Alan Hale *Danker* • Arthur Hoyt *Zeke* • Blanche Frederici *Zeke's wife*

DIRECTOR

Frank Capra

SCREENPLAY

Robert Riskin, from the story *Night Bus* by Samuel Hopkins Adams

AWARDS

Academy Awards (5): Film, Actor (Clark Gable), Actress (Claudette Colbert), Director, Adapted Screenplay

DVD EXTRAS

Columbia Classics: *Frank Capra Remembers* featurette; radio broadcast featuring Clark Gable and Claudette Colbert; vintage advertising gallery; theatrical trailer; filmographies.

QUOTE UNQUOTE

I want to see what love looks like when it's triumphant. I haven't had a good laugh in a week. **PETER WARNE**

IF YOU ENJOYED THIS, WHY NOT TRY ...

The Palm Beach Story (1942)
Sullivan's Travels (1941)

DID YOU KNOW?

Warner Bros animators owed a huge debt to Frank Capra's Oscar-winning film as the scene in which Clark Gable munched on a crrot inspired them to create Bugs Bunny.

The Jerk

CERTIFICATE: **15** | YEAR: **1979** | COUNTRY: **US** | **COLOUR** | RUNNING TIME: **89 MINUTES**

SYNOPSIS

Navin Johnson, the white sheep in a poor black family of Mississippi sharecroppers, leaves home to seek his fortune in the big city. His invention of the Opti-Grab nose support for spectacles and the earth-shattering discovery of his "special purpose" are just part of the Johnson legend.

REVIEW

Has Steve Martin made a funnier film than this comedy of the absurd directed by his then regular collaborator Carl Reiner? His fans will insist that he hasn't, as Martin – in best "manic" mode – takes on the role of a simple-minded and naive southerner, who discovers on his 18th birthday that his family of poor black sharecroppers aren't his natural kith and kin. He takes his dog and leaves the plantation to make his way in a world that is just as loopy as him. There are some heavenly jokes, the standout being the one in which he makes a fortune inventing an absurd nose support for spectacles called the Opti-Grab. In the supporting cast, Bernadette Peters, as the love of his life, and Catlin Adams, as the raunchy motorcycle stunt woman who helps him discover his "special purpose", make telling contributions to the film's wacky nature. **TOM HUTCHINSON**

CAST
Steve Martin *Navin Johnson* • Bernadette Peters *Marie Kimball* • Catlin Adams *Patty Bernstein* • Mabel King *Mother* • Richard Ward *Father* • Dick Anthony Williams *Taj* • Bill Macy *Stan Fox* • M Emmet Walsh *Madman* • Dick O'Neill *Frosty* • Carl Reiner

DIRECTOR
Carl Reiner

SCREENPLAY
Steve Martin, Carl Gottlieb, Michael Elias

DVD EXTRAS
Theatrical trailer; production notes; film highlights.

QUOTE UNQUOTE
You mean I'm gonna *stay* this colour? **NAVIN JOHNSON**

IF YOU ENJOYED THIS, WHY NOT TRY . . .
Being There (1979)
The Man with Two Brains (1983)

DID YOU KNOW?
Dr Strangelove director Stanley Kubrick could often be heard quoting lines from *The Jerk* while he was working.

Kind Hearts and Coronets

CERTIFICATE: **U** | YEAR: **1949** | COUNTRY: **UK** | **BW** | RUNNING TIME: **101 MINUTES**

SYNOPSIS

Louis Mazzini is whiling away the eve of his execution by working on his memoirs. Born the distant heir to a dukedom, he vows to avenge his wronged mother by planning the murder of all the members of her noble family who left her to die in obscurity and who now stand between him and the title he covets.

REVIEW

Arguably the finest of the Ealing comedies, this superb *comédie noire* from director Robert Hamer and producer Michael Balcon has a deliciously witty script that slips smoothly between dastardly deaths in the guise of a self-satisfied memoir. However, the picture is elevated to greatness by the quality of its acting. Obviously, Alec Guinness, who plays the eight doomed D'Ascoynes, merits every superlative lavished on a performance of astounding versatility and virtuosity (he was aged only 35 in this, his first film for the studio). But let's not forget Dennis Price as the ceaselessly inventive killer, and Joan Greenwood and Valerie Hobson as the vamp and the vestal in his life, all of whom are singularly brilliant. Sadly, Hamer, a long-time alcoholic, died penniless in 1963 of pneumonia.

DAVID PARKINSON

CAST

Dennis Price *Louis Mazzini/Narrator* • Valerie Hobson *Edith D'Ascoyne* • Joan Greenwood *Sibella* • Alec Guinness *Duke/Banker/Parson/General/Admiral/Young Ascoyne D'Ascoyne/Young Henry/Lady Agatha D'Ascoyne* • Audrey Fildes *Mama* • Miles Malleson *Hangman* • Clive Morton *Prison governor* • John Penrose *Lionel* • Cecil Ramage *Crown counsel* • Hugh Griffith *Lord High Steward*

DIRECTOR

Robert Hamer

SCREENPLAY

Robert Hamer, John Dighton, from the novel *Israel Rank* by Roy Horniman

DVD EXTRAS

Theatrical trailer; filmographies; photo gallery.

QUOTE UNQUOTE

It is so difficult to make a neat trump of killing people with whom one is not on friendly terms. LOUIS MAZZINI

IF YOU ENJOYED THIS, WHY NOT TRY . . .

No Way to Treat a Lady (1968)
The Ruling Class (1972)
Theatre of Blood (1973)

DID YOU KNOW?

Alec Guinness said that he could hold his breath for four minutes to allow them to show the Admiral's cap floating away. In their delight at the shot, the crew forgot that Guinness's feet were wired to the bottom of the tank and someone had to dive in to cut him free.

The Lady Eve

CERTIFICATE: **U** | YEAR: **1941** | COUNTRY: **US** | **BW** | RUNNING TIME: **89 MINUTES**

SYNOPSIS

Following a long expedition, gauche millionaire and snake enthusiast Charles Pike takes the SS Southern Queen from South America to New York. On board, he catches the eye of beautiful card sharp Jean Harrington who intends to take him for all he's worth. But she doesn't count on falling for her mark.

REVIEW

This wonderfully witty masterpiece was written and directed by the inimitable Preston Sturges. The plot gives a couple of near career-best roles to two of Hollywood's finest, who are perfectly cast here. Henry Fonda plays a wealthy young man obsessed by snakes, who lays himself wide open to the schemes of professional con artist Charles Coburn and his daughter, Barbara Stanwyck. Fonda's buddy, William Demarest, intervenes, but Stanwyck, undeterred, later reappears in disguise at Fonda's palatial manse and tries again. Naturally, the slick, assured sexual opportunist falls for the gauche brewer's son who has spent a year up the Amazon, resulting in a witty, sparkling combination of romance and screwball comedy that is still unequalled. There was a 1956 remake with Mitzi Gaynor called *The Birds and the Bees*, but it didn't come within spitting distance of this great original. **TONY SLOMAN**

CAST

Barbara Stanwyck *Jean Harrington/ Lady Eve Sidwich* • Henry Fonda *Charles Poncefort Pike* • Charles Coburn *"Colonel" Harrington* • Eugene Pallette *Mr Pike* • William Demarest *Muggsy* • Eric Blore *Sir Alfred McGlennan Keith/"Pearly"* • Melville Cooper *Gerald* • Martha O'Driscoll *Martha* • Janet Beecher *Mrs Pike* • Robert Greig *Burrows* • Wilson Benge *Butler*

DIRECTOR

Preston Sturges

SCREENPLAY

Preston Sturges, from the story *The Faithful Heart* by Monckton Hoffe

QUOTE UNQUOTE

They say a moonlit deck is a woman's business office.
JEAN HARRINGTON

IF YOU ENJOYED THIS, WHY NOT TRY ...

Ball of Fire (1941)
Mr Deeds Goes to Town (1936)

DID YOU KNOW?

Barbara Stanwyck was highly impressed by how glamorous Edith Head's costumes made her look in the film. So much so that she repaid the legendary designer by taking her to her dentist so that she could have her teeth fixed.

"The Very Best Larceny
And Old Lace!" —Newsweek

The most hilarious

gangster film

ever made!

The J. ARTHUR RANK Organization
presents

Alec Guinness

as the guiding genius of

The Ladykillers

COLOR BY **TECHNICOLOR**

introducing **KATIE JOHNSON**
with **CECIL PARKER** • **HERBERT LOM**
PETER SELLERS • **DANNY GREEN**

Written by William Rose • Directed by Alexander Mackendrick
A Michael Balcon-Ealing Studios Production
A Continental Distributing Inc. Release

The Ladykillers

CERTIFICATE: **U** | YEAR: **1955** | COUNTRY: **UK** | **COLOUR** | RUNNING TIME: **86 MINUTES**

SYNOPSIS

In order to carry out an audacious robbery, a gang of criminals, posing as musicians, rent rooms in an out-of-the-way house in a nondescript London street. Their flawless plan is hindered, however, by their elderly landlady, Mrs Wilberforce. Now, how to dispose of the sweet but interfering old dear?

REVIEW

A supreme blend of the seedy and the sinister, this was Ealing's last post on the comedy front – indeed, the studio was shutting up shop as this film went on release. Directed by a mischievous Alexander Mackendrick (who made earlier Ealing classics *Whisky Galore!* and *The Man in the White Suit*), this is British comedy at its best, with eccentric characters never for a second seeming out of place in the most everyday locations. Alec Guinness is sublime (and barely recognisable) as the creepy criminal mastermind and his minions (among them Herbert Lom and Peter Sellers) are a marvellous collection of misfits. However, it's the brilliant Katie Johnson as their dotty and unsuspecting landlady, who steals the picture and deservedly earned herself a best actress Bafta at the age of 80. Look out, too, for an early appearance by Frankie Howerd as a narky barrow boy. **DAVID PARKINSON**

CAST

Alec Guinness *Professor Marcus* • Cecil Parker *Major Courtney* • Herbert Lom *Louis* • Peter Sellers *Harry* • Danny Green *One-Round* • Katie Johnson *Mrs Wilberforce* • Jack Warner *Police superintendent* • Philip Stainton *Police sergeant* • Frankie Howerd *Barrow boy* • Kenneth Connor *Cab driver* • Edie Martin *Lettice*

DIRECTOR

Alexander Mackendrick

SCREENPLAY

William Rose, from his story

AWARDS

Baftas (2): British Actress (Katie Johnson), Screenplay

DVD EXTRAS

Theatrical trailer. Also available on Blu-ray.

QUOTE UNQUOTE

One-Round, there is a wheelbarrow outside, could you fetch it? The Major has a train to catch. **PROFESSOR MARCUS**

IF YOU ENJOYED THIS, WHY NOT TRY . . .

A Fish Called Wanda (1988)
Shallow Grave (1994)

DID YOU KNOW?

The producers of *The Ladykillers* vetoed the casting of Katie Johnson as they considered her too frail. Her replacement died before shooting began, so the 80-year-old got the part after all – and won a Bafta.

The Lavender Hill Mob

CERTIFICATE: **U** | YEAR: **1951** | COUNTRY: **UK** | **BW** | RUNNING TIME: **77 MINUTES**

SYNOPSIS

Meek, respectable Henry Holland supervises gold bullion deliveries to the bank where he is a trusted employee. He is seemingly beyond reproach, but behind his modest exterior lurks a criminal mastermind, and, in a south London suburb, Henry hatches an audacious plot to steal a fortune in gold bars.

REVIEW

In this superb and subtle Ealing crime comedy, the inimitable Alec Guinness plays a mild-mannered bank agent who decides to steal £1-million-worth of gold bullion from his employers. Guinness is well supported by the impressive Stanley Holloway, Alfie Bass and Sid James as members of the gang he recruits. Watch out too for a couple of blink-and-miss-them walk-ons from James (billed as William) Fox and Audrey Hepburn, who can be spotted in the opening scene. Director Charles Crichton tips his hat at such genre staples as the studio's own *The Blue Lamp* and the more hard-boiled gangster movies produced by Hollywood in the *film noir* era, and TEB Clarke deservedly won an Oscar for his beautifully constructed story and screenplay. Guinness lost out to Gary Cooper in *High Noon* in the best actor category. **DAVID PARKINSON**

CAST
Alec Guinness *Henry Holland* • Stanley Holloway *Pendlebury* • Sidney James *Lackery* • Alfie Bass *Shorty* • Marjorie Fielding *Mrs Chalk* • John Gregson *Farrow* • Edie Martin *Miss Evesham* • Clive Morton *Station sergeant* • John Salew *Parkin* • Ronald Adam *Turner* • Arthur Hambling *Wallis* • Gibb McLaughlin *Godwin* • Audrey Hepburn *Chiquita* • William Fox [James Fox] *Gregory*

DIRECTOR
Charles Crichton

SCREENPLAY
TEB Clarke

AWARDS
Academy Awards (1): Story and Screenplay
Baftas (1): British Film

DVD EXTRAS
Theatrical trailer.

QUOTE UNQUOTE

I was a potential millionaire, yet I had to be satisfied with eight pounds, fifteen shillings, less deductions. **HENRY HOLLAND**

IF YOU ENJOYED THIS, WHY NOT TRY ...
Gambit (1966)
Topkapi (1964)

DID YOU KNOW?
During a break, Alec Guinness noticed the "fawn-like beauty" of a bit player and told his agent: "I don't know if she can act, but a real film star has just wafted on to the set. Someone should get her under contract." The "fawn" was Audrey Hepburn.

Leningrad Cowboys Go America

CERTIFICATE: **15** | YEAR: **1989** | COUNTRY: **FIN** | **COLOUR** | RUNNING TIME: **75 MINUTES**

SYNOPSIS

In this tale of crazy dreams and crazier hair, The Leningrad Cowboys, the worst band in the world, despair of trying to make the big time in the tundra. Under the iron-fist leadership of their manager, Vladimir, they decide to try their luck in America, where, they hope, people will swallow anything.

REVIEW

Proudly sporting the influence of Jim Jarmusch (who cameos here) on his sleeve, Finnish director Aki Kaurismäki broke out of the art house ghetto and achieved cult status with this scattershot road movie. With their dead bassist travelling in his coffin and their Cadillac brimful of beer cans, the Leningrad Cowboys (whose hairstyles are more pointed than their winklepickers) fulfil their reputation as the world's worst rock band, as they lurch between disastrous Stateside gigs before finally landing in Mexico. Yet, this isn't a *This Is Spinal Tap*-type of picture, as it isn't the Cowboys that are under the microscope, but the deliriously ordinary folk they meet en route. Kaurismäki was back with the band in 1993 for *Leningrad Cowboys Meet Moses* and for the live extravaganza *Total Balalaika Show* in 1994. **DAVID PARKINSON**

CAST
Matti Pellonpaa *Vladimir* • Kari Vaananen *Igor* • Nicky Tesco *Lost cousin* • Jim Jarmusch *Car salesman*

DIRECTOR
Aki Kaurismäki

SCREENPLAY
Aki Kaurismäki

QUOTE UNQUOTE
You know what they say, it is something like, once a cowboy then always a cowboy! **VLADIMIR**

IF YOU ENJOYED THIS, WHY NOT TRY . . .
The Blues Brothers (1980)
Borat: Cultural Learnings of America for Make Benefit Glorious Nation of Kazakhstan (2006)

■

DID YOU KNOW?
Leningrad Cowboys were formed around members of the Finnish band Sleepy Sleepers, who released 19 albums between 1975 and 1989.

Life Is Sweet

CERTIFICATE: **15** | YEAR: **1990** | COUNTRY: **UK** | **COLOUR** | RUNNING TIME: **98 MINUTES**

SYNOPSIS

A working-class couple, Andy and Wendy, living in the London suburb of Enfield, struggle to cope with their own problems as well as those of their twin grown-up daughters. Their friend, Aubrey, has high hopes for a bold new catering venture and Wendy agrees to help out with disastrous results.

REVIEW

Writer/director Mike Leigh is on top form in this superbly observed satire on late-Thatcherite Britain. The wincingly funny and socially astute script (honed by Leigh and his cast at the rehearsal stage) touches on such issues as bulimia, free enterprise and social ambition without ever labouring the point. Alison Steadman and Jim Broadbent are outstanding as the thoroughly decent working-class couple who watch their daughters develop with a mixture of pride and regret. Jane Horrocks does Essex slacker teen with great conviction, while Claire Skinner impresses as her tomboy plumber sister, and Timothy Spall is sweatily repellent as a socially inept, wannabe restaurateur. *Naked* and *Secrets & Lies* won the prizes, but this is perhaps Leigh's finest work – a textbook example of his improvisational style of film-making. **DAVID PARKINSON**

CAST
Alison Steadman *Wendy* • Jim Broadbent *Andy* • Jane Horrocks *Nicola* • Claire Skinner *Natalie* • Stephen Rea *Patsy* • Timothy Spall *Aubrey* • David Thewlis *Nicola's lover* • Moya Brady *Paula* • David Neilson *Steve*

DIRECTOR
Mike Leigh

SCREENPLAY
Mike Leigh

CONTENT ADVICE
Contains swearing, sex scenes, nudity.

QUOTE UNQUOTE
What's nice? It's only a boring cliché. **NICOLA**

IF YOU ENJOYED THIS, WHY NOT TRY ...
High Hopes (1988)
Secrets & Lies (1995)

DID YOU KNOW?
Mike Leigh uses rehearsal and improvisation with his movie casts, and believes in giving them a full background to their characters. So they were respectively introduced to a real-life couple from Enfield, a female plumber, twins and some Arsenal supporters.

Little Miss Sunshine

CERTIFICATE: **15** | YEAR: **2006** | COUNTRY: **US** | **COLOUR** | RUNNING TIME: **98 MINUTES**

SYNOPSIS

When his seven-year-old daughter Olive wins a place in a California beauty pageant, would-be motivational speaker Richard Hoover packs Olive, her heroin-addicted Grandpa, peacemaker mother, mute brother and suicidal uncle into a VW camper van and sets off on what will be a very eventful journey.

REVIEW

Greg Kinnear plays the stressed-out father whose seven-year-old daughter (Abigail Breslin) has been invited to compete in the "Little Miss Sunshine" beauty pageant in this clever swipe at America's obsession with looks and success. He decides to travel the 700 miles to California by road with the rest of his dysfunctional family: resolute wife (Toni Collette), mute son (Paul Dano), suicidal brother-in-law (Steve Carell) and heroin-addled father (Oscar-winning Alan Arkin). Every role is brilliantly cast, but it's a tie for best performance between Kinnear and Carell, who's very good as the Proust scholar unhinged by a failed relationship. Co-directors Jonathan Dayton and Valerie Faris make an impressive feature debut, skilfully balancing the broader humour (involving mislaid porn and a corpse) with genuinely touching drama. **STELLA PAPAMICHAEL**

CAST

Greg Kinnear *Richard* • Steve Carell *Frank* • Toni Collette *Sheryl* • Alan Arkin *Grandpa* • Abigail Breslin *Olive* • Paul Dano *Dwayne*

DIRECTOR

Jonathan Dayton, Valerie Faris

SCREENPLAY

Michael Arndt

AWARDS

Academy Awards (2): Supporting Actor (Alan Arkin), Original Screenplay
Baftas (2): Supporting Actor (Arkin), Original Screenplay

DVD EXTRAS

Commentary by Jonathan Dayton, Valerie Faris and Michael Arndt; four alternative endings with optional commentary by Jonathan Dayton and Valerie Faris. Also available on Blu-ray.

CONTENT ADVICE

Contains swearing, drug abuse.

QUOTE UNQUOTE

There's two kinds of people in this world, there's winners and there's losers. **RICHARD HOOVER**

IF YOU ENJOYED THIS, WHY NOT TRY ...

Drop Dead Gorgeous (1999)
Transamerica (2005)

DID YOU KNOW?

One drive-in screening of the movie was especially for owners of VW camper vans – 65 of them turned up for the event.

Local Hero

CERTIFICATE: **PG** | YEAR: **1983** | COUNTRY: **UK** | **COLOUR** | RUNNING TIME: **107 MINUTES**

SYNOPSIS

A young American oil executive is sent to a small Scottish village that his company intends to use as the location for a new refinery. While attempting to negotiate with the local community, he finds himself unexpectedly outmanoeuvred – but is still irresistibly drawn to the ruggedly beautiful area.

REVIEW

Chariots of Fire producer David Puttnam was the executive behind this charming comedy drama, which firmly established Bill Forsyth as a major British film-maker after his equally whimsical *Gregory's Girl*. It's a lyrical, almost mystical tale that follows the attempts of billionaire Texas oilman Burt Lancaster and his minion Peter Riegert to buy up an isolated Scottish village in order to build an oil refinery. But they haven't bargained on the village's integral strength of community, which is encapsulated by hermit Fulton Mackay, whose family, it turns out, has owned the local beach for four centuries, and he won't be the one to sell it. Cinematographer Chris Menges takes full advantage of the stunning scenery, the performances are funny, ironic and moving (Lancaster, in particular, is superb as the eccentric tycoon), and Forsyth brings a sure directorial touch to the proceedings. **SIMON ROSE**

CAST

Peter Riegert *MacIntyre* • Burt Lancaster *Happer* • Denis Lawson *Urquhart* • Peter Capaldi *Oldsen* • Fulton Mackay *Ben* • Jenny Seagrove *Marina* • Jennifer Black *Stella* • Christopher Asante *Reverend MacPherson* • Rikki Fulton *Geddes*

DIRECTOR

Bill Forsyth

SCREENPLAY

Bill Forsyth

AWARDS

Baftas (1): Director

DVD EXTRAS

Interview with writer and director Bill Forsyth.

CONTENT ADVICE

Contains swearing.

QUOTE UNQUOTE

How do you do business with a man who has no door?
MACINTYRE

IF YOU ENJOYED THIS, WHY NOT TRY ...

Gregory's Girl (1980)
Whisky Galore! (1949)

DID YOU KNOW?

The beach and village used as locations in the film are actually on opposite coasts of Scotland.

Lost in Translation

CERTIFICATE: **15** | YEAR: **2003** | COUNTRY: **US** | **COLOUR** | RUNNING TIME: **97 MINUTES**

SYNOPSIS

World-weary 50-something movie star Bob Harris is in Tokyo, shooting a whisky commercial "for the money". In his hotel, he meets the unhappy Charlotte, a recent philosophy graduate in her 20s who's trapped in a loveless marriage to a photographer, and the two lost souls forge a deep bond.

REVIEW

You'd never guess from Bill Murray's delicately restrained and masterful performance in this sad, funny, magical and almost irresistibly moving romantic comedy drama that he is the same actor who spent decades making broad comedies such as *Ghost Busters* and *Caddyshack*. He stars as a jaded actor reluctantly staying in Japan to make a whisky commercial, who meets and begins to fall in love with an unhappily married younger woman (played by the equally good Scarlett Johansson). Writer/director Sofia Coppola – who won an Oscar for her screenplay – expertly uses the neon-drenched backdrop of night-time Tokyo as an alien landscape against which the couple delicately explore each other's ambiguous feelings, and wisely underpins the bittersweet soul-searching with a healthy dose of humour. ADAM SMITH

CAST

Bill Murray *Bob Harris* • Scarlett Johansson *Charlotte* • Giovanni Ribisi *John* • Anna Faris *Kelly* • Fumihiro Hayashi *Charlie* • Catherine Lambert *Jazz singer* • Akiko Takeshita *Ms Kawasaki*

DIRECTOR

Sofia Coppola

SCREENPLAY

Sofia Coppola

AWARDS

Academy Awards (1): Original Screenplay
Baftas (3): Actor (Bill Murray), Actress (Scarlett Johansson), Editing

DVD EXTRAS

Lost On Location behind-the-scenes featurette; *Matthew's Best Hit TV* extended scenes; *City Girl* music video from Kevin Shields; conversation with Sofia Coppola and Bill Murray; theatrical trailer.

QUOTE UNQUOTE

You're probably just having a midlife crisis. Did you buy a Porsche yet? CHARLOTTE

IF YOU ENJOYED THIS, WHY NOT TRY ...

Avanti! (1972)
Two for the Road (1967)

DID YOU KNOW?

Sofia Coppola wrote the film for Bill Murray but, with only a verbal commitment, she had no idea if he was going to show up. Murray recalls: "This is the only time that anyone's ever written something that I was so eager to do... I guess I'm a hopeless romantic."

■

117

Love and Death

CERTIFICATE: **PG** | YEAR: **1975** | COUNTRY: **US** | **COLOUR** | RUNNING TIME: **81 MINUTES**

SYNOPSIS

In the early 19th century, Boris, a pacifist and reluctant Russian army conscript, finds himself an unwitting hero after single-handedly destroying an enemy position. After marrying his sweetheart, Sonja, she browbeats him into conceiving a plot to assassinate Napoleon and end the war in Europe.

REVIEW

You never know where Woody Allen is coming from. With homages to Sergei Eisenstein and Bob Hope – among others – this off-the-wall satire is located in the fatalistic Russian territory of *War and Peace*. In 1812 a condemned Allen ("all men go eventually, but I go at six o'clock tomorrow morning. I was supposed to go at five o'clock, but I have a smart lawyer.") looks back in bemusement at the historical events, and a hysterical Diane Keaton, that have brought him to his execution. The Grim Reaper scythes through from *The Seventh Seal*, but the jokes are strictly New York Jewish and delightfully anachronistic. The use of Sergei Prokofiev's joyous music is also an inspired choice for one of the best of Allen's "early, funny" movies, where the quick-fire verbal and visual gags never fail to hit their mark.

TOM HUTCHINSON

CAST

Woody Allen *Boris* • Diane Keaton *Sonja* • Georges Adet *Old Nehamkin* • Frank Adu *Drill sergeant* • Edmond Ardisson *Priest* • Feodor Atkine *Mikhail*

DIRECTOR

Woody Allen

SCREENPLAY

Woody Allen, Sergei Prokofiev

DVD EXTRAS

Theatrical trailer.

QUOTE UNQUOTE

If it turns out that there is a God, I don't think that he's evil. I think that the worst you can say about him is that basically he's an underachiever. **BORIS**

IF YOU ENJOYED THIS, WHY NOT TRY ...

Sleeper (1973)
Take the Money and Run (1969)

DID YOU KNOW?

While filming in Hungary, Woody Allen existed on the tinned food and bottled water that he had brought from the United States.

■

The Man in the White Suit

CERTIFICATE: **U** | YEAR: **1951** | COUNTRY: **UK** | **BW** | RUNNING TIME: **81 MINUTES**

SYNOPSIS

The seemingly haphazard experiments of eccentric scientist Sidney Stratton have a far-reaching effect on the textile industry when he invents an indestructible cloth that never gets dirty. Management don't want the mills shut down, the unions agree with them for once and washerwomen are furious...

REVIEW

Telling the story of an idealistic young scientist who is undone by the seeming perfection of his own invention, this astute film from director Alexander Mackendrick is the only Ealing comedy to truly bare its teeth. Capitalist greed, professional jealousy, the spectre of unemployment and a fear of progress are just some of the provocative themes explored in this razor-sharp satire that spurns the studio's customary whimsy. Adapted from a play by Mackendrick's cousin, Roger MacDougal, it stars Alec Guinness as wonderfully unworldly boffin Sidney Stratton, whose indestructible cloth unites the textile industry against him. Guinness gives one of his best Ealing performances, but Joan Greenwood is perhaps even more impressive as Daphne, the spirited daughter of mill owner Alan Birnley (Cecil Parker). **DAVID PARKINSON**

CAST

Alec Guinness *Sidney Stratton* • Joan Greenwood *Daphne Birnley* • Cecil Parker *Alan Birnley* • Michael Gough *Michael Corland* • Ernest Thesiger *Sir John Kierlaw* • Vida Hope *Bertha* • Howard Marion-Crawford *Cranford* • Miles Malleson *Tailor* • Henry Mollison *Hoskins*

DIRECTOR

Alexander Mackendrick

SCREENPLAY

Roger MacDougall, John Dighton, Alexander Mackendrick, from the play by Roger MacDougall

DVD EXTRAS

Theatrical trailer.

QUOTE UNQUOTE

Some fool has invented an indestructible cloth. Where is he? How much does he want? **SIR JOHN KIERLAW**

IF YOU ENJOYED THIS, WHY NOT TRY ...

Modern Times (1936)
Tucker: the Man and His Dream (1988) ∎

DID YOU KNOW?

Produced using tuba and bassoon notes, the noise emitted by the chemistry apparatus was later set to music and released as *The White Suit Samba*. It was performed by Jack Parnell and His Rhythm, and produced by Beatles collaborator George Martin.

The Man with Two Brains

CERTIFICATE: **15** | YEAR: **1983** | COUNTRY: **US** | **COLOUR** | RUNNING TIME: **85 MINUTES**

SYNOPSIS

Brain surgeon Dr Michael Hfuhruhurr uses his pioneering skills to save the beautiful but deadly Dolores Benedict following a car accident. The two are soon married, but not happily so, and he finds himself falling in love with a disembodied brain in a jar. Who will he choose, beauty or the brain?

REVIEW

Steve Martin may have been more madcap in *The Jerk*, and produced a more accomplished performance in *Roxanne*, but this dazzling comedy remains his finest hour. As the unpronounceable Doctor Hfuhruhurr, he gets to read his favourite poem ("Pointy birds, oh pointy pointy, Anoint my head, anointy nointy"), carry out a citizen's divorce and endure the world's toughest drink-driving test, while Kathleen Turner hilariously sends up the *femme fatale* persona that she established in *Body Heat*. There's also David Warner as a mad scientist (whose hotel apartment fittingly resembles a gothic castle), an uncredited Sissy Spacek voicing brain in a jar Anne Uumellmahaye, and a surprise cameo in the form of the Elevator Killer. It's all sublimely entertaining, and a reminder of Martin's too-often neglected comic genius. **JOHN FERGUSON**

CAST
Steve Martin *Dr Michael Hfuhruhurr* • Kathleen Turner *Dolores Benedict* • David Warner *Dr Necessiter* • Paul Benedict *Butler* • Richard Brestoff *Dr Pasteur* • James Cromwell *Realtor* • George Furth *Timon* • Peter Hobbs *Dr Brandon* • Earl Boen *Dr Conrad* • Sissy Spacek *Anne Uumellmahaye*

DIRECTOR
Carl Reiner

SCREENPLAY
Steve Martin, Carl Reiner, George Gipe

CONTENT ADVICE
Contains some violence, swearing, brief nudity.

QUOTE UNQUOTE

Brains! I've never seen so many brains out of their heads before. I feel like a kid in a candy store. **DR MICHAEL HFUHRUHURR**

IF YOU ENJOYED THIS, WHY NOT TRY ...

All of Me (1984)
Bride of Frankenstein (1935)

■

DID YOU KNOW?
Steve Martin studied philosophy at university and used the subject for much of his material as a stand-up comedian in the 1970s.

Manhattan

CERTIFICATE: **15** | YEAR: **1979** | COUNTRY: **US** | **BW** | RUNNING TIME: **92 MINUTES**

SYNOPSIS

TV comedy writer and would-be novelist Isaac Davis is 42 years old and unsure about his relationship with 17-year-old high school student Tracy. He's also falling for Mary, the highly strung mistress of his best friend Yale, and facing the humiliation of a tell-all book by his lesbian ex-wife.

REVIEW

Setting the tone and style for many of his later movies, this early masterpiece from Woody Allen celebrates, as ever, his beloved New York. Allen stars as a neurotic middle-aged writer who's taken up with a teenage student (Mariel Hemingway), but who's being diverted by the fast-talking mistress (Diane Keaton) of his best friend and – more dangerously – by the book about him written by his lesbian ex-wife (Meryl Streep). Allen's characters swan in and out of the cultural byways of the Big Apple, indulging in psychiatric therapy that's never quite the cure-all they crave. They could have become over-articulate bores, but the wonder of Allen is that he manages to invest them with the saving grace of humanity. This is a great film, with beautiful black and white photography by Gordon Willis and a George Gershwin score that adds just the right amount of poignancy. **TOM HUTCHINSON**

CAST

Woody Allen *Isaac Davis* • Diane Keaton *Mary Wilke* • Michael Murphy *Yale* • Mariel Hemingway *Tracy* • Meryl Streep *Jill* • Anne Byrne *Emily* • Karen Ludwig *Connie* • Michael O'Donoghue *Dennis* • Wallace Shawn *Jeremiah*

DIRECTOR

Woody Allen

SCREENPLAY

Woody Allen, Marshall Brickman

AWARDS

Baftas (2): Film, Screenplay

DVD EXTRAS

Theatrical trailer.

CONTENT ADVICE

Contains swearing.

QUOTE UNQUOTE

Chapter One. He was as tough and romantic as the city he loved. **ISAAC DAVIS**

IF YOU ENJOYED THIS, WHY NOT TRY . . .

Annie Hall (1977)
Mighty Aphrodite (1995)

DID YOU KNOW?

Actress Stacey Nelkin, who dated Woody Allen while she was at high school in New York, is said to be the inspiration for Mariel Hemingway's character Tracy. Nelkin had a role in Allen's *Bullets over Broadway* in 1994.

MASH

CERTIFICATE: **15** | YEAR: **1969** | COUNTRY: **US** | **COLOUR** | RUNNING TIME: **110 MINUTES**

SYNOPSIS

Surgeons Hawkeye Pierce and Trapper John McIntyre are posted to the 4077th Mobile Army Surgical Hospital in Korea at the height of the conflict, where gallows humour and practical jokes help relieve the tension as medical staff await the arrival of front-line casualties and battle army bureaucracy.

REVIEW

The quality of this acerbic study of life in a Korean War field hospital is often overlooked because of the popularity of the TV series it spawned. Fans of the series may take a while to get used to Donald Sutherland in the role of Hawkeye that Alan Alda later made his own; similarly, Sally Kellerman is less well known as "Hot Lips" than Loretta Swit, who played the character on TV. But the glorious wit of Ring Lardner Jr's Oscar-winning script soon has you under its spell. Sutherland and Elliott Gould as Trapper give beautifully understated performances, and are totally believable as surgeons – so much so that you never doubt the medical patter as they deal with the grisly procession of casualties. Director Robert Altman and Kellerman each received one of the five Oscar nominations, as did the film for best picture – it lost out to flag-waving biopic *Patton*. **DAVID PARKINSON**

QUOTE UNQUOTE

Follow the zany antics of our combat surgeons as they cut and stitch their way along the front lines, operating as bombs... operating as bombs and bullets burst around them; snatching laughs and love between amputations and penicillin. **PA ANNOUNCER**

IF YOU ENJOYED THIS, WHY NOT TRY ...

Catch-22 (1970)

CAST

Donald Sutherland *Hawkeye Pierce* • Elliott Gould *Trapper John McIntyre* • Tom Skerritt *Duke Forrest* • Sally Kellerman *Major "Hot Lips" Houlihan* • Robert Duvall *Major Frank Burns* • Jo Ann Pflug *Lieutenant Dish* • René Auberjonois *Dago Red* • Roger Bowen *Colonel Henry Blake* • Gary Burghoff *Radar O'Reilly*

DIRECTOR

Robert Altman

SCREENPLAY

Ring Lardner Jr, from the novel by Richard Hooker

AWARDS

Academy Awards (1): Adapted Screenplay
Baftas (1): UN Award

DVD EXTRAS

Special Edition: commentary by Robert Altman; *MASH Backstory*: behind-the-scenes featurette; *Enlisted: the story of MASH*; *MASH - Comedy under Fire* documentary; 30th anniversary cast reunion; theatrical trailer.

CONTENT ADVICE

Contains swearing, brief nudity.

DID YOU KNOW?

Robert Altman's 14-year-old son, Mike, wrote the lyrics for the theme song *Suicide Is Painless* and was said to have made more money than his dad.

Midnight Run

CERTIFICATE: **18** | YEAR: **1988** | COUNTRY: **US** | **COLOUR** | RUNNING TIME: **121 MINUTES**

SYNOPSIS

Bounty hunter Jack Walsh is just the man to bring Jonathan "Duke" Mardukas to justice. The $100,000 fee is just what Jack needs right now – the only problem is that Jonathan cheated the Mafia out of a cool $15 million, and they want it back. Can Jack beat the FBI and a rival to his quarry?

REVIEW

Robert De Niro played this action picture for laughs and, as a result, had his first hit in years. Made by Martin Brest, director of the original *Beverly Hills Cop*, it's a variant on that film's odd-couple theme, as De Niro's foul-mouthed bounty hunter Jack Walsh goes on the run with an accountant called Jonathan Mardukas, who has embezzled $15 million from the Mob. Mardukas is portrayed by Charles Grodin, whose underplaying is an absolute joy: he looks like a puppy that's lost its poop tray. As with all the best road movies – and this is one of the best – the picture really moves, as a simple air trip from New York to Los Angeles turns into a saga of trains and automobiles, car crashes, and skirmishes with the FBI and a dozen other interested parties. There may be similarities to *Beverly Hills Cop*, but the characters here are definitely more interesting.

ADRIAN TURNER

CAST

Robert De Niro *Jack Walsh* • Charles Grodin *Jonathan Mardukas* • Yaphet Kotto *Alonzo Mosely* • John Ashton *Marvin Dorfler* • Dennis Farina *Jimmy Serrano* • Joe Pantoliano *Eddie Moscone* • Richard Foronjy *Tony Darvo*

DIRECTOR

Martin Brest

SCREENPLAY

George Gallo

DVD EXTRAS

Filmographies; theatrical trailer.

CONTENT ADVICE

Contains swearing, violence.

QUOTE UNQUOTE

You're OK, Jack. I think... under different circumstances you and I probably still would have hated each other!

JONATHAN MARDUKAS

IF YOU ENJOYED THIS, WHY NOT TRY ...

48 HRS (1982)
The 39 Steps (1935)

DID YOU KNOW?

Charles Grodin spent so much time handcuffed in the film, mostly to co-star Robert De Niro, that he developed scars around his wrists.

Monsieur Hulot's Holiday

CERTIFICATE: **U** | YEAR: **1953** | COUNTRY: **FR** | **BW** | RUNNING TIME: **83 MINUTES**

SYNOPSIS

Jacques Tati's second film introduced his most popular character, the blundering but well-meaning Monsieur Hulot, who takes a holiday and disrupts the tranquillity of a quiet seaside resort. Hulot is a gentle soul, but chaos seems to have taken a liking to him and follows, comically, in his wake.

REVIEW

Inspired by the sophisticated silent clowning of Max Linder and Buster Keaton, Jacques Tati's masterpiece is a sublime blend of satire, slapstick and character comedy that was itself a key influence on the *nouvelle vague*. With the genial Hulot invariably at its centre, much of the hilarious seaside action was filmed in long shot at the Brittany resort of St Marc-sur-Mer. This was not only to allow the gags to develop in their own time and space, but also enabled audiences to discover for themselves Tati's intuitive use of the film frame, his acute understanding of human behaviour, and his gently mocking appreciation of the absurdities and inefficiencies of the modern world. It was nominated for a best screenplay Oscar and was named as the best film of all time by director Richard Lester (*A Hard Day's Night*) in a 2002 *Sight and Sound* poll. **DAVID PARKINSON**

CAST

Jacques Tati *Monsieur Hulot* • Nathalie Pascaud *Martine* • Michèle Rolla *Aunt* • Raymond Carl *Waiter* • Lucien Frégis *Hotel proprietor* • Valentine Camax *Englishwoman*

DIRECTOR

Jacques Tati

SCREENPLAY

Jacques Tati, Henri Marquet, Pierre Aubert, Jacques Lagrange

DVD EXTRAS

Interview with director Richard Lester; theatrical trailers.

DID YOU KNOW?

Tati was voted the 46th greatest director of all time by the magazine *Entertainment Weekly*, even though he's only credited with directing nine films in his career.

IF YOU ENJOYED THIS, WHY NOT TRY ...

Mr Bean's Holiday (2007)
Mon Oncle (1958)

■

Monty Python and the Holy Grail

CERTIFICATE: **15** | YEAR: **1975** | COUNTRY: **UK** | **COLOUR** | RUNNING TIME: **85 MINUTES**

SYNOPSIS

King Arthur and his page Patsy are seeking knights to join them at Camelot's Round Table. But a more demanding task surfaces when God himself instructs them to seek the Holy Grail. Many perils await the questers, such as the Knights Who Say Ni, rude Frenchmen and the ultra-combative Black Knight.

REVIEW

Complete with some inspired digressions and shorn of some of the weaker sketches, the soundtrack album of the Pythons' first story-based feature is even funnier than the film itself. Yet this remains a wonderfully inventive comedy that brilliantly debunks the Dark Ages and legends of chivalry through King Arthur's encounters with an anarcho-syndicalist commune, the Black Knight, God (courtesy of Terry Gilliam) and the "knights who say ni". The *Camelot* and *Sir Robin* songs also get beneath the visor, but the highlights are the trial of Connie Booth's witch and the Holy Hand Grenade of Antioch sequence. Shame about the ending, though – apparently, a conclusion in which King Arthur and his knights find the Holy Grail in Harrods department store was abandoned and the production ran out of money before a suitable substitute could be found. **DAVID PARKINSON**

CAST

Graham Chapman *King Arthur* • John Cleese *Black Knight/Sir Lancelot* • Terry Gilliam *Patsy/Green Knight* • Eric Idle *Sir Robin/Brother Maynard* • Terry Jones *Dennis' mother/Sir Bedevere* • Michael Palin *Dennis/Sir Galahad* • Connie Booth *Witch*

DIRECTOR

Terry Gilliam, Terry Jones

SCREENPLAY

Graham Chapman, John Cleese, Terry Gilliam, Eric Idle, Terry Jones, Michael Palin

DVD EXTRAS

Extraordinarily Deluxe Edition: commentary by Terry Gilliam and Terry Jones; commentary by John Cleese, Eric Idle and Michael Palin; two on location featurettes; singalong; *Follow the Killer Rabbit* featurette; *How to Use Your Coconuts* educational film; new documentary; theatrical trailers; photo gallery; spoof trailer based on *The Da Vinci Code*.

CONTENT ADVICE

Contains swearing, some violence, nudity.

QUOTE UNQUOTE

If you do not tell us where we can buy a shrubbery, my friend and I will say... we will say... "ni". **KING ARTHUR**

IF YOU ENJOYED THIS, WHY NOT TRY ...

Jabberwocky (1977)
Time Bandits (1981)

DID YOU KNOW?

The inspired idea for the team to mime horse-riding while their porters followed them banging coconut shells together only came about because using real horses was beyond the film's budget.

Monty Python's Life of Brian

CERTIFICATE: **15** | YEAR: **1979** | COUNTRY: **UK** | **COLOUR** | RUNNING TIME: **89 MINUTES**

SYNOPSIS

Mistaken for Jesus from the moment of his birth, when the three wise men visit the wrong manger, Brian is destined to go through life in the shadow of the true Messiah. The adult Brian embarks on an anti-Roman crusade that sees him branded a prophet by the people and a troublemaker by the authorities.

REVIEW

This inspired send-up of religious epics was surrounded by controversy on its release, but it is, nevertheless, the Monty Python team's most assured and satisfying cinematic work. Graham Chapman is the Judaean whose life bears some resemblance to that of a certain carpenter around the same time, although the shambling story serves mainly as an excuse for the assembled Pythons to take pot shots at some of their favourite targets and serve up some joyfully juvenile gags. Michael Palin has some of the choicest roles, including the Roman governor with a speech impediment ("Welease Wodewick") and a disgruntled ex-leper. There's also a very funny and quite irrelevant cameo from Spike Milligan, plus a blink-and-you'll-miss-him appearance from ex-Beatle George Harrison, whose financial backing rescued the troubled production. **JOHN FERGUSON**

QUOTE UNQUOTE

He's not the Messiah. He's a very naughty boy.
THE MOTHER OF BRIAN, A RATBAG

IF YOU ENJOYED THIS, WHY NOT TRY ...

History of the World Part 1 (1981)
Monty Python's The Meaning of Life (1983)

CAST

Terry Jones *The Virgin Mandy/The mother of Brian, a ratbag/Colin/Simon the holy man/Saintly passer-by* • Graham Chapman *First Wise Man/Brian called Brian/Biggus Dickus* • Michael Palin *Second Wise Man/Mr Big Nose/Francis, a Revolutionary/Mrs A, who casts the second stone/Ex-leper/Ben, an ancient prisoner/ Pontius Pilate, Roman governor/A boring prophet/Eddie/Nisus Wettus* • John Cleese *Third Wise Man/Reg, leader of the Judean People's Front/Jewish official at the stoning/Centurion of the Yard/Deadly Dirk/Arthur* • Eric Idle *Mr Cheeky/Stan called Loretta, a confused revolutionary/Harry the Haggler, beard and stone salesman/Culprit Woman, who casts the first stone/Intensely dull youth/Otto, the Nazarene jailer's assistant/Mr Frisbee III* • Terry Gilliam *Another person further forward/ Revolutionaries and masked commandos/A blood and thunder prophet/Geoffrey/Jailer*

DIRECTOR

Terry Jones

SCREENPLAY

Graham Chapman, John Cleese, Terry Gilliam, Eric Idle, Terry Jones, Michael Palin

DVD EXTRAS

Two-disc Immaculate Edition: commentary Terry Jones, Michael Palin, Eric Idle. John Cleese and Terry Gilliam; documentary; deleted scenes; radio spots; original script read-through; photo gallery. Also available on Blu-ray.

CONTENT ADVICE

Contains violence, swearing, nudity.

DID YOU KNOW?

The decision by Norwegian authorities to ban the film proved a godsend to advertisers across the border in Sweden where it was billed as, "The film too funny to be shown in Norway."

The Naked Gun

CERTIFICATE: **15** | YEAR: **1988** | COUNTRY: **US** | **COLOUR** | RUNNING TIME: **81 MINUTES**

SYNOPSIS

After a violent confrontation with some of America's most reviled enemies, deadpan detective Lt Frank Drebin joins his colleagues in a special unit to protect Queen Elizabeth II on her visit to Los Angeles. But Drebin is soon sidetracked when his partner is shot while chasing a gang of drug smugglers.

REVIEW

The team behind *Airplane!* first turned their wicked talents onto the police force with the short-lived cult TV series *Police Squad!*, but it was this hilarious feature-length spoof that introduced Leslie Nielsen's inspired Frank Drebin to a worldwide audience. Nielsen remains wonderfully stone-faced as the inept lieutenant, who wreaks havoc in LA around the time of a visit by Queen Elizabeth II. The supporting players – George Kennedy as his captain, Priscilla Presley as the equally clumsy love interest and OJ Simpson as the wounded colleague – are also delightfully deadpan, and the determinedly juvenile gags never stop flowing. Highlights include the the Queen at a Dodgers' baseball game and Frank forgetting to turn his surveillance microphone off when he goes to the toilet. **JOHN FERGUSON**

QUOTE UNQUOTE

It's the same old story. Boy finds girl, boy loses girl, girl finds boy, boy forgets girl, boy remembers girl, girls dies in a tragic blimp accident over the Orange Bowl on New Year's Day. **LIEUTENANT FRANK DREBIN**

IF YOU ENJOYED THIS, WHY NOT TRY ...

Airplane! (1980)
Hot Fuzz (2007)

CAST

Leslie Nielsen *Lieutenant Frank Drebin* • Priscilla Presley *Jane Spencer* • Ricardo Montalban *Vincent Ludwig* • George Kennedy *Captain Ed Hocken* • OJ Simpson *Nordberg* • Nancy Marchand *Mayor*

DIRECTOR

David Zucker

SCREENPLAY

Jerry Zucker, Jim Abrahams, David Zucker, Pat Proft, from the TV series *Police Squad!* by David Zucker, Jerry Zucker, Jim Abrahams

DVD EXTRAS

Audio commentary by David Zucker and Robert Weiss (producer).

CONTENT ADVICE

Contains swearing.

DID YOU KNOW?

Peter Noone of Herman's Hermits was asked to perform a new version of the band's 1964 number one hit *I'm into Something Good* as the directors wanted the song speeded up.

National Lampoon's Animal House

CERTIFICATE: **15** | YEAR: **1978** | COUNTRY: **US** | **COLOUR** | RUNNING TIME: **108 MINUTES**

SYNOPSIS

At Faber College in 1962, the students of Delta House fraternity have a reputation for wild parties and drinking. However, as the latest batch of freshmen arrives on campus, the future of the house comes under threat from the dean, who has decided that such unbridled behaviour is not to be tolerated.

REVIEW

It spawned a number of puerile spin-offs, but this cheerfully vulgar offering deserves the status of comedy classic. As well as providing John Belushi with his best ever role, it also helped launch the career of a number of rising young actors (Kevin Bacon, Tom Hulce, Peter Riegert), not to mention director John Landis and co-writer Harold Ramis, who was a colleague of Belushi's in television comedy sketch show *Second City* in the mid-1970s. There's not much of a plot to speak of: at a US college in the early 1960s, dean John Vernon plots to remove the depraved Delta House fraternity from the campus; Belushi and his fellow students decide to fight back. Everyone remembers the food fight, but the film is crammed with smart sight gags and one-liners, and Belushi's incomprehensible rallying speech at the end is quite wonderful. **JOHN FERGUSON**

QUOTE UNQUOTE

Over? Did you say over? Nothing is over until we decide it is. Was it over when the Germans bombed Pearl Harbor? Hell no! **JOHN "BLUTO" BLUTARSKY**

IF YOU ENJOYED THIS, WHY NOT TRY ...

Old School (2003)
Porky's (1981)

CAST

John Belushi *John "Bluto" Blutarsky* • Tim Matheson *Eric "Otter" Stratton* • John Vernon *Dean Vernon Wormer* • Verna Bloom *Marion Wormer* • Thomas Hulce [Tom Hulce] *Larry "Pinto" Kroger* • Peter Riegert *Donald "Boon" Schoenstein* • Stephen Furst *Kent "Flounder" Dorfman* • Kevin Bacon *Chip Diller*

DIRECTOR

John Landis

SCREENPLAY

Harold Ramis, Douglas Kenney, Chris Miller

DVD EXTRAS

Special Edition: "Where Are They Now" featurette; music video; animated anecdotes; "The Yearbook": an *Animal House* reunion; theatrical trailer. Also available on Blu-ray.

CONTENT ADVICE

Contains swearing, nudity.

DID YOU KNOW?

Director John Landis sacrificed his distinctive beard and much of his hair to play a cafeteria dishwasher who encounters Belushi's Bluto character. However, though it was filmed, his sacrifice was in vain as the scene didn't make it into the final cut.

A Night at the Opera

CERTIFICATE: **U** | YEAR: **1935** | COUNTRY: **US** | **BW** | RUNNING TIME: **87 MINUTES**

SYNOPSIS

Otis B Driftwood must get wealthy Mrs Claypool to invest her money in an opera, so she can break into high society. Meanwhile, unknown tenor Riccardo Baroni battles for recognition, with the help of friend and agent Fiorello, as his soprano girlfriend is whisked off to fame and fortune in New York.

REVIEW

This first Marx Brothers outing for MGM was honed on stage, but producer Irving G Thalberg used the three-week pre-production tour to chip away at the rough edges that made the siblings' humour so unique. Yet, despite his determination to make them conform to the studio's polished brand of entertainment, their anarchic spirit triumphs. Consequently, the plotline involving Groucho's bid to introduce wealthy Margaret Dumont into society through opera is almost an irrelevance. Certainly the romantic interludes with songbirds Allan Jones and Kitty Carlisle are. But the madcap lunacy is unforgettable – whether it's the shenanigans inside Groucho's cabin on a transatlantic liner; or Groucho's inimitable line in patter (particularly while attempting to schmooze Dumont and negotiate a contract with Chico); or the slapstick ruination of *Il Trovatore*. This is a true comedy classic. **DAVID PARKINSON**

CAST

Groucho Marx *Otis B Driftwood* • Chico Marx *Fiorello* • Harpo Marx *Tomasso* • Margaret Dumont *Mrs Claypool* • Allan Jones *Riccardo Baroni* • Kitty Carlisle *Rosa Castaldi* • Siegfried "Sig" Rumann [Sig Ruman] *Herman Gottlieb*

DIRECTOR

Sam Wood

SCREENPLAY

George S Kaufman, Morrie Ryskind, Al Boasberg, Bert Kalmar, Harry Ruby, from a story by James Kevin McGuinness

DVD EXTRAS

The Marx Brothers Collection six-disc boxed set: commentary by Leonard Maltin; documentary *Remarks on Marx*; Groucho Marx on the *Hy Gardner Show*; vintage MGM shorts *Sunday Night at the Trocadero* and *How to Sleep*.

QUOTE UNQUOTE

When I invite a woman to dinner I expect her to look at my face. That's the price she has to pay. **OTIS B DRIFTWOOD**

IF YOU ENJOYED THIS, WHY NOT TRY ...

The Big Store (1941)
A Night in Casablanca (1946)

DID YOU KNOW?

This was the first comedy the team made without Zeppo. The straight man in their movies, he was naturally witty offscreen and became a successful Hollywood agent. He was also the inventor of a clamping device used by US bombers to drop the atomic bomb.

Ninotchka

CERTIFICATE: **U** | YEAR: **1939** | COUNTRY: **US** | **BW** | RUNNING TIME: **105 MINUTES**

SYNOPSIS

Comrade Ninotchka is sent to Paris to investigate the dubious activities of a Soviet trade delegation. After a chance meeting with the sauve aristocrat Count d'Algout, the stern commissar is soon embracing the capitalist way of life and discovering that love is more than a mere chemical reaction.

REVIEW

This is one of the funniest, most original screen comedies ever made, and from the greatest year in Hollywood's history. Director Ernst Lubitsch brings his magic touch to bear on an inspired screenplay by Billy Wilder, Charles Brackett and Walter Reisch about a Soviet emissary (played by the great Greta Garbo) sent to Paris to retrieve three errant communists who have fallen in love with the ways of the West. Of course, it's just a matter of time before Garbo melts and falls in love, in her case with debonair count Melvyn Douglas. Witty, sophisticated, immaculately cast and superbly performed, this film was advertised in its day simply as "Garbo laughs!". That she does, and so will you, long and loud, especially at the utterly charming café scene. It was remade in 1957 with music as *Silk Stockings*, but this original is much the better of the two. **TONY SLOMAN**

CAST

Greta Garbo *Ninotchka, Nina Ivanova Yakushova* • Melvyn Douglas *Count Leon d'Algout* • Ina Claire *Grand Duchess Swana* • Bela Lugosi *Commissar Razinin* • Sig Rumann [Sig Ruman] *Iranoff* • Felix Bressart *Buljanoff* • Alexander Granach *Kopalski* • Gregory Gaye *Count Alexis Rakonin*

DIRECTOR

Ernst Lubitsch

SCREENPLAY

Charles Brackett, Billy Wilder, Walter Reisch, from a story by Melchior Lengyel

QUOTE UNQUOTE

Don't make an issue of my womanhood. **COMRADE NINOTCHKA**

IF YOU ENJOYED THIS, WHY NOT TRY ...

One, Two, Three (1961)
Silk Stockings (1957)

DID YOU KNOW?

Greta Garbo was terrified of doing the drunk scene and put off shooting it until the end of the production. Not only did she disapprove of alcohol, but she was also ashamed of appearing intoxicated in front of other actors.

■

143

The Odd Couple

CERTIFICATE: **PG** | YEAR: **1968** | COUNTRY: **US** | **COLOUR** | RUNNING TIME: **101 MINUTES**

SYNOPSIS

When Felix Ungar's marriage breaks up, his carefree friend Oscar Madison invites him to share the squalor of his apartment. But when the neurotic, domesticated Felix gives the place the "Good Housekeeping Seal of Approval", Oscar is determined that one of them will go, and it won't be him.

REVIEW

In this film version of Neil Simon's celebrated play, television journalist Felix Ungar (Jack Lemmon), devastated by the break-up of his marriage, packs his sinuses and his nervous tics and moves in with happily divorced sports writer Oscar Madison (Walter Matthau). While Felix is the finicky housewife (crustless sandwiches, coasters for drinks, nifty hoover technique), Oscar is the arch slob (brimming ashtrays, unmade bed, linguini on the walls), and they inevitably drive each other nuts. Apart from a cringe-making scene featuring two English girls, this comedy has weathered well, and it bristles with one-liners timed to perfection by the two leads. Matthau and Lemmon returned for a belated sequel in 1998, and a TV series based on the film starring Tony Randall as Felix and Jack Klugman as Oscar ran for five years in the 1970s. **DAVID PARKINSON**

CAST

Jack Lemmon *Felix Ungar* • Walter Matthau *Oscar Madison* • John Fiedler *Vinnie* • Herb Edelman *Murray* • David Sheiner *Roy* • Larry Haines *Speed* • Monica Evans *Cecily* • Carole Shelley *Gwendolyn*

DIRECTOR

Gene Saks

SCREENPLAY

Neil Simon, from his play

DVD EXTRAS

Theatrical trailer.

QUOTE UNQUOTE

I got, uh, brown sandwiches and, uh, green sandwiches. Which one do you want? **OSCAR MADISON**

IF YOU ENJOYED THIS, WHY NOT TRY ...

Grumpy Old Men (1993)
The Sunshine Boys (1975)

DID YOU KNOW?

Danny Simon was inspired to write this story after he moved in with an agent friend to reduce expenses after their divorces. But he became blocked and his brother took on the project, receiving sole authorial credit. Following its huge success, Neil Simon gave a percentage to his sibling.

Passport to Pimlico

CERTIFICATE: **U** | YEAR: **1949** | COUNTRY: **UK** | **BW** | RUNNING TIME: **80 MINUTES**

SYNOPSIS

When a bomb left over from the war finally explodes, it leads to the discovery that a small area of south London is historically part of Burgundy, France. New borders are drawn up, a government is formed and the local inhabitants look forward to a continental lifestyle free from postwar austerity.

REVIEW

This cosy Ealing comedy set in the aftermath of the Second World War is essentially a one-joke affair spun out with masterly skill by that gifted teller of shaggy-dog stories, TEB Clarke, who received an Oscar nomination. When an explosion uncovers hidden treasure and an ancient document, historian Margaret Rutherford discovers that the Pimlico area of London belongs to the Duchy of Burgundy. The locals duly declare independence and Pimlico becomes an affluent oasis in the austerity hit capital. Given this set-up, the scene could have been set for a sniping satire on the state of postwar England. In the event, Clarke and director Henry Cornelius cock only the gentlest of snooks at such bugbears as rationing and the breakdown of wartime camaraderie, but as most of the situations are ingenious, this is the only minor disappointment in what is a memorable exploration of the British character. **DAVID PARKINSON**

QUOTE UNQUOTE

It's just because we are English that we're sticking up for our rights to be Burgundians. **CONNIE PEMBERTON**

IF YOU ENJOYED THIS, WHY NOT TRY . . .

The Mouse That Roared (1959)
The Titfield Thunderbolt (1952)

CAST

Stanley Holloway *Arthur Pemberton* • Margaret Rutherford *Professor Hatton-Jones* • Basil Radford *Gregg* • Naunton Wayne *Straker* • Hermione Baddeley *Edie Randall* • John Slater *Frank Huggins* • Betty Warren *Connie Pemberton* • Barbara Murray *Shirley Pemberton*

DIRECTOR

Henry Cornelius

SCREENPLAY

TEB Clarke

DVD EXTRAS

Theatrical trailer.

DID YOU KNOW?

A radio announcer refers to Latin music performed by "Les Norman and his Bethnal Green Bambinos", a joke at the expense of producer (and Barry Norman's father) Leslie Norman.

The Philadelphia Story

CERTIFICATE: **U** | YEAR: **1940** | COUNTRY: **US** | **BW** | RUNNING TIME: **107 MINUTES**

SYNOPSIS

The preparations for the wedding of socialite Tracy Lord to self-made man George Kittredge are turned upside down by the arrival of playboy CK Dexter Haven – Lord's first husband – who brings with him two reluctant employees of *Spy* magazine, Macaulay "Mike" Connor and Liz Imbrie.

REVIEW

Fans of the musical remake *High Society* who haven't seen this classic, all-talking, no-dancing original might wish to remedy that. In order to reverse her reputation as "box-office poison", Katharine Hepburn shrewdly bought the rights to the Broadway play (written for her by Philip Barry) in which she had been a hit. With old pal George Cukor as director and a hand-picked cast, this film was a success. In it, her society girl is engaged to John Howard's executive dullard; her ex-husband Cary Grant turns up with information about an imminent press scandal, while a rival publication's reporter James Stewart finds his class-war cynicism melting away as he falls for Hepburn. There's a lot more to it than that, of course – so take your chance to view this as soon as possible to enjoy romantic comedy at its most sublime. **ANDREW COLLINS**

CAST

Cary Grant *CK Dexter Haven* • Katharine Hepburn *Tracy Samantha Lord* • James Stewart *Macaulay "Mike" Connor* • Ruth Hussey *Elizabeth Imbrie* • John Howard *George Kittredge* • Roland Young *Uncle Willie* • John Halliday *Seth Lord* • Mary Nash *Margaret Lord* • Virginia Weidler *Dinah Lord* • Henry Daniell *Sidney Kidd*

DIRECTOR

George Cukor

SCREENPLAY

Donald Ogden Stewart, from the play by Philip Barry

AWARDS

Academy Awards (2): Actor (James Stewart), Screenplay

DVD EXTRAS

Two-disc Special Edition: commentary by film historian Jeannine Basinger; gallery of George Cukor trailers; *Katharine Hepburn: All about Me: a Self Portrait*; *The Men Who Made the Movies: George Cukor* documentary; two radio adaptations featuring three stars of the movie (audio only)

QUOTE UNQUOTE

I thought all writers drank to excess and beat their wives. You know, one time, I secretly wanted to be a writer.
CK DEXTER HAVEN

IF YOU ENJOYED THIS, WHY NOT TRY . . .

High Society (1956)
My Best Friend's Wedding (1997)

DID YOU KNOW?

Katharine Hepburn wanted Spencer Tracy or Clark Gable to play CK Dexter Haven. But director George Cukor insisted on hiring her three-time co-star Cary Grant, who promptly gave his $125,000 fee to British War Relief Charities.

Pink Flamingos

CERTIFICATE: **18** | YEAR: **1972** | COUNTRY: **US** | **COLOUR** | RUNNING TIME: **100 MINUTES**

SYNOPSIS

Trailer-dwelling drag queen Divine is the proud possessor of the title "Filthiest Person Alive". When Raymond and Connie Marbles challenge her crown, it's a fight to the disgusting death involving chicken sex, a singing rectum, artificial insemination, baby trafficking and ingested dog poo.

REVIEW

This is the film that not only defined bad taste, but also unashamedly celebrated it. Cult director John Waters's notorious gross-out (his third feature and the first shot in colour) has upstart perverts David Lochary and Mink Stole trying to wrest the honour of "Filthiest Person Alive" from the tenacious grip of sleaze superstar Divine. Chicken sex, a singing rectum, artificial insemination, lesbian motherhood and the incomparable Edith Massey are paraded before our increasingly appalled eyes in the "Prince of Puke's" screamingly funny shocker. Featuring the infamous coda where Divine eats dog excrement (for real), Waters's unique obscenity is the grandfather of midnight movies. Reputedly shot on a budget of only $12,000, it grossed around $10 million worldwide and consolidated the career of its director. **ALAN JONES**

CAST
Divine *Babs Johnson/Divine* • David Lochary *Raymond Marble* • Mary Vivian Pearce *Cotton* • Mink Stole *Connie Marble* • Danny Mills *Crackers* • Edith Massey *Mama Edie* • Channing Wilroy *Channing* • Cookie Mueller *Cookie*

DIRECTOR
John Waters

SCREENPLAY
John Waters

CONTENT ADVICE
Contains sex scenes, swearing, violence.

QUOTE UNQUOTE

Kill everyone now! Condone first degree murder! Advocate cannibalism! Eat s**t! Filth is my politics! Filth is my life!
BABS JOHNSON

IF YOU ENJOYED THIS, WHY NOT TRY . . .

Female Trouble (1974)
Polyester (1981)

DID YOU KNOW?
In one of the longest-ever opening credits sequences, all the actors and extras in the movie are listed.

Play It Again, Sam

CERTIFICATE: **15** | YEAR: **1972** | COUNTRY: **US** | **COLOUR** | RUNNING TIME: **81 MINUTES**

SYNOPSIS

When his wife leaves him, insecure film critic Allan Felix asks married friends Dick and Linda to set him up on dates. But when he needs tips on how to romance these women, he turns to his idol, Humphrey Bogart, who appears to Allan in spirit form with some snappy advice about the fundamental things.

REVIEW

Adapted by Woody Allen from his 1969 stage play, this is one of the few films that America's leading auteur has not directed himself. That task fell to Herbert Ross, who adopts a rather overcautious approach to the story. But such is the calibre of the playing and the assurance of the writing that it's almost impossible to resist. Allen plays film buff Allan Felix, who's trying to pick up the pieces and rejoin the dating game after being dumped by his wife. He's obsessed by Humphrey Bogart and calls on the spirit of the great actor for advice on how to treat women. Eventually, after many disasters, he embarks on a tentative relationship with Diane Keaton, the wife of his workaholic best friend Tony Roberts. The more politically correct may feel their hackles rise from time to time, but the one-liners here are among Allen's best and the Bogart allusions are priceless.

DAVID PARKINSON

CAST

Woody Allen *Allan Felix* • Diane Keaton *Linda Christie* • Tony Roberts *Dick Christie* • Jerry Lacy *Humphrey Bogart* • Susan Anspach *Nancy Felix* • Jennifer Salt *Sharon* • Joy Bang *Julie* • Viva *Jennifer*

DIRECTOR

Herbert Ross

SCREENPLAY

Woody Allen, from his play

QUOTE UNQUOTE

I love the rain – it washes memories off the sidewalk of life. **ALLAN FELIX**

IF YOU ENJOYED THIS, WHY NOT TRY ...

Casablanca (1942)
Dead Men Don't Wear Plaid (1982)

DID YOU KNOW?

When New York film workers went on strike in the summer of 1971, production was moved to San Francisco, making this one of the few Woody Allen films to be shot away from the Big Apple.

The Player

CERTIFICATE: **15** | YEAR: **1992** | COUNTRY: **US** | **COLOUR** | RUNNING TIME: **119 MINUTES**

SYNOPSIS

Hollywood film executive Griffin Mill is on top – for now. He's under pressure at work, has a younger colleague snapping at his well-shod heels and is receiving death threats in the post. Suspecting that a spurned screenwriter is trying to ruin him, Mill goes to great lengths to protect his career.

REVIEW

From its masterly eight-minute opening crane shot to the final blockbuster pastiche, this swingeing satire is easily the best movie about Tinseltown since *Sunset Blvd.* Director Robert Altman turns the spotlight on the industry hands that feed him and scores a bullseye on each target. The temptation is to play spot the star, but don't let the galaxy of cameos from such celebrities as Bruce Willis, Julia Roberts and Cher distract from the gloriously cynical plot and a towering turn from a marvellously oily Tim Robbins. He merited at least an Oscar nomination for his performance as Griffin Mill, the high-flying studio executive who is troubled by poison-pen postcards from a discarded scriptwriter, the ambitions of wunderkind Peter Gallagher and the snooping of cop Whoopi Goldberg, who suspects him of murder. This is Hollywood at its worst told by Hollywood at its best. **DAVID PARKINSON**

CAST

Tim Robbins *Griffin Mill* • Greta Scacchi *June Gudmundsdottir* • Fred Ward *Walter Stuckel* • Whoopi Goldberg *Detective Susan Avery* • Peter Gallagher *Larry Levy* • Brion James *Joel Levison* • Cynthia Stevenson *Bonnie Sherow* • Vincent D'Onofrio *David Kahane* • Dean Stockwell *Andy Civella* • Richard E Grant *Tom Oakley* • Sydney Pollack *Dick Mellen*

DIRECTOR

Robert Altman

SCREENPLAY

Michael Tolkin, from his novel

AWARDS

Baftas (2): Director, Adapted Screenplay

DVD EXTRAS

One on one with Robert Altman; deleted scenes; commentary by Robert Altman and Michael Tolkin; theatrical trailer.

CONTENT ADVICE

Contains violence, swearing, nudity.

QUOTE UNQUOTE

Can we talk about something other than Hollywood for a change? We're educated people. **GRIFFIN MILL**

IF YOU ENJOYED THIS, WHY NOT TRY . . .

The Big Picture (1989)
Get Shorty (1995)

DID YOU KNOW?

The handwriting on the death-threat postcards is Robert Altman's.

Pleasantville

CERTIFICATE: **12** | YEAR: **1998** | COUNTRY: **US** | **COLOUR AND BW** | RUNNING TIME: **119 MINUTES**

SYNOPSIS

After a fight over the TV remote control, two teenagers find themselves transported to the black-and-white setting of 1950s soap opera *Pleasantville*. While struggling to fit in, the siblings discover that their modern sensibilities are having a strange effect on the show's characters.

REVIEW

Tobey Maguire and Reese Witherspoon play sparring siblings who, while fighting over the TV remote control, get zapped inside Maguire's favourite soap, a 1950s re-run called "Pleasantville". They find themselves in what is literally a black-and-white world – a time-warped tellyplace where the the men do all the work and where a woman's place isn't just in the home, it's in the kitchen. How the youngsters' progressive attitude to sex and marriage begins to induce unfamiliar feelings in the show's two-dimensional caricatures forms the basis of this witty and affectionate comedy. And how these new-found emotions are depicted by the gradual encroachment of colour into their monochrome lives is where its brilliance lies. It's a clever concept, beautifully acted by a top-notch cast that includes Joan Allen, William H Macy and Jeff Daniels. **DAVE ALDRIDGE**

CAST

Tobey Maguire *David* • Reese Witherspoon *Jennifer* • Joan Allen *Betty Parker* • William H Macy *George Parker* • Jeff Daniels *Mr Johnson* • JT Walsh *Big Bob* • Don Knotts *TV repairman*

DIRECTOR

Gary Ross

SCREENPLAY

Gary Ross

DVD EXTRAS

Commentary by Gary Ross; *The Art of Pleasantville* featurette; *Across the Universe* music video; theatrical trailer; cast and crew biographies.

CONTENT ADVICE

Contains swearing.

QUOTE UNQUOTE

Listen, why don't you take this remote instead? It's got a little more oomph in it. **TV REPAIRMAN**

IF YOU ENJOYED THIS, WHY NOT TRY . . .

Peggy Sue Got Married (1986)
The Purple Rose of Cairo (1985)

DID YOU KNOW?

As director Gary Ross shot the whole of the film in colour, he had to use an unprecedented 1,700 digital effects to create the various monochrome images littered throughout the film.

The Producers

CERTIFICATE: **PG** | YEAR: **1968** | COUNTRY: **US** | **COLOUR** | RUNNING TIME: **84 MINUTES**

SYNOPSIS

Once the "King of Broadway", Max Bialystock is now making a living by conning old ladies out of their savings to finance his doomed productions. His accountant, Leo Bloom, mentions a sure-fire way of making some quick cash by putting on a guaranteed flop – and a hideous new musical is born.

REVIEW

This triumphantly tasteless affair was Mel Brooks's first feature and it fully deserves its status as a comedy classic. Zero Mostel plays sweaty, down-on-his-luck Broadway impresario Max Bialystock, who links up with shy accountant Leo Bloom (Gene Wilder) in a scam to fleece theatrical investors with the worst play of all time: a musical biopic of Adolf Hitler. The two leads are wonderful, as are Dick Shawn as hippy star Lorenzo St Du Bois ("LSD"), who takes the lead role in their production, and Kenneth Mars as their unhinged neo-Nazi playwright Franz Liebkind. The gags flow freely throughout, but it's the jaw-dropping numbers from *Springtime for Hitler* (with lyrics like "Don't be stupid, be a smarty, come and join the Nazi Party") that cement the film's place in cinema history. JOHN FERGUSON

QUOTE UNQUOTE

Will the dancing Hitlers please wait in the wings? We are only seeing singing Hitlers. ROGER DE BRIS

IF YOU ENJOYED THIS, WHY NOT TRY . . .

Bullets over Broadway (1994)
The Tall Guy (1989)
To Be or Not to Be (1983)

CAST

Zero Mostel *Producer* • Gene Wilder *Leo Bloom* • Kenneth Mars *Franz Liebkind* • Estelle Winwood *"Hold me, touch me" old lady* • Renee Taylor *Eva Braun* • Christopher Hewett *Roger De Bris* • Lee Meredith *Ulla* • Andreas Voutsinas *Carmen Giya* • Dick Shawn *Lorenzo St Du Bois* • Josip Elic *Violinist* • Madlyn Cates *Concierge* • John Zoller *Drama critic* • William Hickey *Drunk in theatre bar*

DIRECTOR

Mel Brooks

SCREENPLAY

Mel Brooks

AWARDS

Academy Awards (1): Original Story and Screenplay

DVD EXTRAS

Special Edition: "making of" featurette; outtakes; sketch gallery; theatrical trailer.

DID YOU KNOW?

Mel Brooks allowed Dustin Hoffman (his original Franz Liebkind) to audition for *The Graduate* as Brooks had read the script (his wife, Anne Bancroft, was to play Mrs Robinson) and thought Hoffman totally wrong for the tall, blond-haired role!

Raising Arizona

CERTIFICATE: **12** | YEAR: **1987** | COUNTRY: **US** | **COLOUR** | RUNNING TIME: **90 MINUTES**

SYNOPSIS

Inveterate crook Hi McDonnough turns his back on a life of crime to marry Edwina, a police officer he meets on his regular journeys to jail. Their happiness is marred only by their inability to have children, so when they hear that quintuplets have been born nearby they set out to steal one.

REVIEW

This delirious mix of slapstick, surrealism and sentimentality from Joel and Ethan Coen is one of their warmest and most complete works. Nicolas Cage and Holly Hunter play a couple who decide to kidnap one of a set of famous Arizona quintuplets when they discover they can't have children, only to find themselves pursued by the lone biker of the apocalypse. Cage and Hunter (in her breakthrough role) are superb, and there are winning supporting performances from John Goodman and William Forsythe as two cons on the run. However, in the end it is the dazzling invention of the Coen brothers that shines through. Excepting the technical wizardry that created Jim Carrey's *The Mask*, this is probably the closest anyone will ever get to a live-action Tex Avery cartoon – from the audacious pre-credits sequence, the pace never slackens for a second.
JOHN FERGUSON

CAST
Nicolas Cage *Hi McDonnough* • Holly Hunter *Edwina* • Trey Wilson *Nathan Arizona Sr* • John Goodman *Gale* • William Forsythe *Evelle* • Frances McDormand *Dot*

DIRECTOR
Joel Coen

SCREENPLAY
Ethan Coen, Joel Coen

DVD EXTRAS
Theatrical trailer.

CONTENT ADVICE
Contains violence, swearing.

QUOTE UNQUOTE
Edwina's insides were a rocky place where my seed could find no purchase. **HI MCDONNOUGH**

IF YOU ENJOYED THIS, WHY NOT TRY ...
Crimewave (1985)
The Sugarland Express (1974)

DID YOU KNOW?
A number of babies were used to play the Arizona quintuplets in the film, possibly because some were fired as soon as they began to walk. "They'd make the walk of shame," quipped Ethan Coen.

The Royal Tenenbaums

CERTIFICATE: **15** | YEAR: **2001** | COUNTRY: **US** | **COLOUR** | RUNNING TIME: **105 MINUTES**

SYNOPSIS

Royal Tenenbaum is the estranged father of three gifted children whose promise foundered as adults. A once successful lawyer, Royal is now broke and homeless. Feigning terminal illness, he is taken back into the family home by his long-suffering wife Etheline, and one-by-one the children return.

REVIEW

Produced and directed by the hugely talented Wes Anderson and co-written with regular collaborator Owen Wilson, this is the much anticipated follow-up to *Rushmore*, one of the quirkier American films of the late 1990s. *The Royal Tenenbaums* is no less quirky. An ambitiously original ensemble comedy, it is related in an episodic, storybook format with off-screen narration from Alec Baldwin. This stylised presentation suggests that the interlocking subplots involving the various Tenenbaums – Gwyneth Paltrow's foundering marriage to Bill Murray; Ben Stiller's paranoia; Luke Wilson's deepening depression – will be resolved in a detached fashion, without the audience's empathy. That is not so. As the narrative builds, the atmosphere thaws and something like poetry unfolds. Immaculately written and brilliantly performed, this extraordinary fable restores one's faith in American cinema. **ANDREW COLLINS**

CAST

Gene Hackman *Royal Tenenbaum* • Anjelica Huston *Etheline Tenenbaum* • Ben Stiller *Chas Tenenbaum* • Gwyneth Paltrow *Margot Tenenbaum* • Owen Wilson *Eli Cash* • Bill Murray *Raleigh St Clair* • Danny Glover *Henry Sherman* • Luke Wilson *Richie Tenenbaum* • Alec Baldwin *Narrator*

DIRECTOR

Wes Anderson

SCREENPLAY

Wes Anderson, Owen Wilson

DVD EXTRAS

With the Film-maker - portraits by Albert Maysles; behind-the-scenes and interviews with cast and crew; *The Art of the Movie*; outtakes; theatrical trailers.

QUOTE UNQUOTE

I'm sorry for your loss. Your mother was a terribly attractive woman. **ROYAL TENENBAUM**

IF YOU ENJOYED THIS, WHY NOT TRY ...

The Addams Family (1991)
The Darjeeling Limited (2007)

DID YOU KNOW?

The opening segment of *The Royal Tenenbaums*, in which narrator Alec Baldwin gives a potted history of the family's crises and achievements, was a homage to a similar sequence in Orson Welles's 1942 masterpiece *The Magnificent Ambersons*.

Rushmore

CERTIFICATE: **15** | YEAR: **1998** | COUNTRY: **US** | **COLOUR** | RUNNING TIME: **89 MINUTES**

SYNOPSIS

Fifteen-year-old Max Fischer is an underachieving student and king of the after-school club. His studies suffer still further when he becomes smitten with teacher Rosemary Cross and finds that he has a rival for her hand in the shape of eccentric millionaire and school benefactor Herman Blume.

REVIEW

This unusual black comedy from writer/director Wes Anderson and co-writer Owen Wilson (*Bottle Rocket, The Royal Tenenbaums*) centres on an extremely unconventional teen hero. The boy in question is 15-year-old Max Fischer (Jason Schwartzman), one of the least popular pupils at the exclusive Rushmore Academy, who nonetheless runs just about every club and school activity in a megalomaniacal effort to further himself. Schwartzman gives a superbly nerdy performance, but Bill Murray – playing a depressed millionaire who strikes up a friendship with Max – steals every scene. However, the pair's new-found bond is soon threatened when they both fall for a widowed teacher (Olivia Williams). This is a quirky, edgy and very funny tale about a young outsider who just might end up leading all those who laugh at him. **JOANNA BERRY**

CAST

Jason Schwartzman *Max Fischer* • Bill Murray *Herman Blume* • Olivia Williams *Rosemary Cross* • Brian Cox *Dr Guggenheim* • Seymour Cassel *Bert Fischer* • Mason Gamble *Dirk Calloway* • Owen Wilson *Edward Applebee*

DIRECTOR

Wes Anderson

SCREENPLAY

Wes Anderson, Owen Wilson

CONTENT ADVICE

Contains swearing.

QUOTE UNQUOTE

Maybe I'm spending too much of my time starting up clubs and putting on plays. I should probably be trying harder to score chicks. **MAX FISCHER**

IF YOU ENJOYED THIS, WHY NOT TRY ...

Election (1999)
The Royal Tenenbaums (2001)

DID YOU KNOW?

The photos of Rosemary's dead husband are actually of actor Owen Wilson, who co-wrote the film.

The School of Rock

CERTIFICATE: **PG** | YEAR: **2003** | COUNTRY: **US/GER** | COLOUR | RUNNING TIME: **104 MINUTES**

SYNOPSIS

An out-of-work heavy metal guitarist cons his way into a supply-teaching job at an expensive private school. Introducing the uptight students to the joys of rock music, Finn sets about grooming them for a battle-of-the-bands contest that could solve his money problems – unless he gets found out.

REVIEW

The School of Rock is that rare thing: a kid's film that doesn't patronise its target audience and has enough wit also to entertain adults. Jack Black is outstanding as Dewey Finn, an unemployed rock guitarist who passes himself off as a supply teacher and enlightens the sheltered pupils of a posh private school with the joys of rock 'n' roll. Joan Cusack provides excellent comic support as the school's headmistress who is twitchily uptight but by no means unsympathetic. Director Richard Linklater (the indie darling who brought us *Slacker* and *Dazed and Confused*) deftly avoids the schmaltz and pre-programmed plotlines that can easily ruin these kinds of films. He extracts not one, but more than half a dozen enjoyable, natural performances from his young cast. This is expertly crafted escapism as well as a near-perfect family movie. ADAM SMITH

CAST

Jack Black *Dewey Finn* • Joan Cusack *Principal Rosalie Mullins* • Mike White *Ned Schneebly* • Sarah Silverman *Patty Di Marco* • Joey Gaydos Jr *Zack* • Maryam Hassan *Tomika* • Miranda Cosgrove *Summer* • Kevin Clark *Freddy*

DIRECTOR

Richard Linklater

SCREENPLAY

Mike White

DVD EXTRAS

Commentary by Jack Black and Richard Linklater; commentary by the kids; Jack Black and kids' video diaries; Jack Black's pitch to Led Zeppelin; music video; *Dewey Finn's History of Rock* featurette.

QUOTE UNQUOTE

Dude, I service society by rocking, OK? I'm out there on the front lines liberating people with my music! DEWEY FINN

IF YOU ENJOYED THIS, WHY NOT TRY ...

Bandslam (2009)
Tenacious D in The Pick of Destiny (2006) ∎

DID YOU KNOW?

Screenwriter Mike White created the character of Dewey Finn for Jack Black having lived next door to him (and his loud rock music) for three years.

A Romantic Comedy.
With Zombies.
SHAUN OF THE DEAD
ROGUE PICTURES, STUDIO CANAL AND WORKING TITLE FILMS PRESENT
A WT2 PRODUCTION IN ASSOCIATION WITH BIG TALK PRODUCTIONS "SHAUN OF THE DEAD" SIMON PEGG
KATE ASHFIELD LUCY DAVIS NICK FROST DYLAN MORAN BILL NIGHY PENELOPE WILTON JINA JAY DANIEL MUDFORD AND PETE WOODHEAD
RONALDO VASCONCELLOS ANNIE HARDINGE MARCUS ROWLAND CHRIS DICKENS DAVID M. DUNLAP TIM BEVAN ERIC FELLNER
NATASCHA WHARTON JAMES WILSON ALISON OWEN SIMON PEGG AND EDGAR WRIGHT NIRA PARK EDGAR WRIGHT
R
For Zombie Violence/Gore And Language
STUDIO CANAL
ROGUE PICTURES
www.shaunofthedeadmovie.com
This September aim for the head.

Shaun of the Dead

CERTIFICATE: **15** | YEAR: **2004** | COUNTRY: **UK/US/FR** | **COLOUR** | RUNNING TIME: **95 MINUTES**

SYNOPSIS

On the day north London slacker Shaun finally decides to sort his life out, the dead rise and the city becomes overrun with zombies. Can Shaun and his best mate Ed fight off the marauding hordes of the undead and at the same time win back Shaun's girlfriend? Or will they just go down the pub?

REVIEW

If you like Simon Pegg and director Edgar Wright's cult Channel 4 series *Spaced*, you'll enjoy this deadpan blend of undergraduate humour and hardcore horror, which ransacks George A Romero's *Dead* saga (Londoner Shaun is forced to fight the undead as the capital becomes Zombie Central) along with virtually every Italian zombie flick for inspiration. It may seem like a one-joke conceit, but you do actually care about the characters, which sustains the narrative. Shaun's mates are all played by familiar TV faces – *Spaced's* Nick Frost, *The Office's* Lucy Davis, Dylan Moran from *Black Books*. But the real stars are his mum, the magnificent Penelope Wilton, and stepdad, Bill Nighy, who move the splatter farce into more resonant areas. Proof – along with their follow-up pastiche *Hot Fuzz* – that British film comedy can work without Richard Curtis.

ALAN JONES

QUOTE UNQUOTE

Oh, for God's sake! He's got an arm off! SHAUN

IF YOU ENJOYED THIS, WHY NOT TRY ...

An American Werewolf in London (1981)
Hot Fuzz (2007)
Tremors (1989)

CAST

Simon Pegg *Shaun* • Kate Ashfield *Liz* • Nick Frost *Ed* • Dylan Moran *David* • Lucy Davis *Dianne* • Penelope Wilton *Barbara* • Bill Nighy *Philip* • Jessica Stevenson *Yvonne*

DIRECTOR

Edgar Wright

SCREENPLAY

Edgar Wright, Simon Pegg

DVD EXTRAS

Commentaries by Simon Pegg, Nick Frost, Edgar Wright and all leading cast members; commentary by the zombies; outtakes; video diaries; make-up tests; trailers; poster designs; TV spots; *Potholes* comic strip sequence; photo gallery.

CONTENT ADVICE

Contains violence, swearing.

DID YOU KNOW?

George A Romero (who directed the zombie classic *Night of the Living Dead* and its sequels) is a huge fan of this British spoof of his movies, and invited director Edgar Wright and star Simon Pegg to cameo as zombies in his 2005 follow-up *Land of the Dead*.

Shrek & Shrek 2

CERTIFICATE: **U** | YEAR: **2001/2004** | COUNTRY: **US** | **COLOUR** | RUNNING TIME: **86 MINUTES**

SYNOPSIS

In the first of these animated fantasies, Shrek, a grumpy green ogre, agrees to rescue a princess in return for having his swamp cleared of fairy-tale characters, and is joined on his mission by a talking donkey. The adventures continue in the sequel, which adds Puss in Boots to the mythical mix.

REVIEW

These brilliant animated fantasy comedies from DreamWorks are irreverent, occasionally scatological fairy tales about an antisocial green ogre called Shrek (Mike Myers). In the first, he sets out with a talking donkey (a scene-stealing Eddie Murphy) to rescue a princess called Fiona (Cameron Diaz) in order to rid his swamp of an infestation of fairy-tale characters (whose disrespectful treatment suggests a sly dig at Disney). The sequel details his trip to Far Far Away to meet Fiona's parents, King Harold (John Cleese) and Queen Lillian (Julie Andrews), and his run-in with assassin Puss-in-Boots (Antonio Banderas). The animators achieve a startling level of reality, but it's the characterisations and wild invention that carry the stories. The parodies, pop references and Hollywood send-ups are hilarious, and the subtle satire and double entendres can be enjoyed by young and old alike.

ANDREW COLLINS/ALAN JONES

QUOTE UNQUOTE

You might have seen a housefly, maybe even a superfly, but I bet you ain't never seen a donkey fly. **DONKEY**

IF YOU ENJOYED THIS, WHY NOT TRY . . .

The Princess Bride (1987)
Shrek the Third (2007)

CAST

Mike Myers *Shrek/Blind mouse* • Eddie Murphy *Donkey* • Cameron Diaz *Princess Fiona* • John Lithgow *Lord Farquaad* • Julie Andrews *Queen Lillian* • Antonio Banderas *Puss-in-Boots* • John Cleese *King Harold* • Rupert Everett *Prince Charming* • Jennifer Saunders *Fairy Godmother* • Vincent Cassel *Monsieur Hood*

DIRECTOR

Andrew Adamson, Vicky Jenson, Kelly Asbury, Conrad Vernon

SCREENPLAY

J David Stem, Andrew Adamson, David N Weiss, Ted Elliott, Terry Rossio, Joe Stillman, Roger SH Schulman, from a book by William Steig

AWARDS

Academy Awards (Shrek) (1): Animated Feature
Baftas (Shrek) (1): Adapted Screenplay

DVD EXTRAS

Double disc package: *Shrek*: interactive games; character interviews; trivia game; design the gingerbread man; karaoke dance party. *Shrek 2: Far Far Away Idol* – vote for your favourite character; 11 songs.

DID YOU KNOW?

Shrek was supposed to be voiced by *Saturday Night Live* star Chris Farley. He'd even recorded some dialogue when he died of a drug overdose in 1997 at the age of 33. The role went to Mike Myers.

Sideways

CERTIFICATE: **15** | YEAR: **2004** | COUNTRY: **US** | **COLOUR** | RUNNING TIME: **121 MINUTES**

SYNOPSIS

With the nuptials of his best friend Jack approaching, wine connoisseur and failing writer Miles decides to take him on a road trip through California's wine country. The pair have very different ideas of an appropriate send-off: Miles wants to sample fine vintages, while Jack wants a final fling.

REVIEW

Alexander Payne's gloriously picaresque analysis of midlife crises does exactly as the title suggests. It takes oblique glances at the buddy flick and road movie, and skewers both with poignancy, truth and wit to give a fresh vitality to each well-worn genre. This dissection of American social mores follows the misadventures of middle-aged mates Miles (Paul Giamatti) and Jack (Thomas Haden Church) on their trip to California's wine country to celebrate the latter's upcoming wedding. The performances of Giamatti (a rumpled bundle of nervous self-loathing), Church (a deliciously deadpan but fading Casanova) and Virginia Madsen (a grape-savvy waitress) are spot on, and help make this a richly rewarding comedy of the finest vintage. Nominated for five Oscars including best film and direction, it won for Payne and Jim Taylor's screenplay, but deserved a lot more. **ALAN JONES**

QUOTE UNQUOTE

If you don't have money at my age, you're not even in the game anymore. You're just a pasture animal waiting for the abattoir. **MILES RAYMOND**

IF YOU ENJOYED THIS, WHY NOT TRY . . .

The Hangover (2009)
Harvey (1950)

CAST

Paul Giamatti *Miles Raymond* • Thomas Haden Church *Jack Lopate* • Virginia Madsen *Maya* • Sandra Oh *Stephanie* • Marylouise Burke *Miles's mother* • Jessica Hecht *Victoria* • Missy Doty *Cammi* • MC Gainey *Cammi's husband*

DIRECTOR

Alexander Payne

SCREENPLAY

Alexander Payne, Jim Taylor, from the novel by Rex Pickett

AWARDS

Academy Awards (1): Adapted Screenplay
Baftas (1): Adapted Screenplay

DVD EXTRAS

Commentary by Paul Giamatti and Thomas Haden Church; behind-the-scenes featurette; deleted scenes with introductions; hidden features.

CONTENT ADVICE

Contains swearing, sex scenes.

DID YOU KNOW?

Director Alexander Payne selected the film's wine list himself.

Sleeper

CERTIFICATE: **PG** | YEAR: **1973** | COUNTRY: **US** | **COLOUR** | RUNNING TIME: **83 MINUTES**

SYNOPSIS

When meek jazz musician Miles Monroe finally comes round from a minor operation, he discovers that he's been in cryogenic suspension for 200 years. To the totalitarian government of 2174 he's a dangerous relic, to the freedom fighters he's a symbol of resistance, but mostly he's still a coward.

REVIEW

In this silly but often hilarious comedy, Woody Allen plays a jazz musician who comes round from what he thinks was a minor operation only to discover that he has been in cryogenic suspension for 200 years and that it is now 2174. What follows is partly inspired by *1984* (Allen becomes involved with revolutionaries opposing the totalitarian government), but mainly a homage to great screen comedians of the past, among them Charlie Chaplin, Buster Keaton and Harry Langdon. The sight gags include some of the funniest things Allen's ever done (in particular, the scene in which he's disguised as a robot) and there's a rich quota of brilliantly witty lines throughout. In her second film with Allen after the previous year's *Play It Again, Sam*, Diane Keaton makes a fine foil. **DAVID MCGILLIVRAY**

CAST
Woody Allen *Miles Monroe* • Diane Keaton *Luna Schlosser* • John Beck *Erno Windt* • Marya Small *Dr Nero* • Bartlett Robinson *Dr Orva* • Mary Gregory *Dr Melik* • Chris Forbes *Rainer Krebs*

DIRECTOR
Woody Allen

SCREENPLAY
Woody Allen, Marshall Brickman

DVD EXTRAS
Theatrical trailer.

CONTENT ADVICE
Contains swearing.

QUOTE UNQUOTE

I'm not the heroic type. Really, I was beaten up by Quakers. **MILES MONROE**

IF YOU ENJOYED THIS, WHY NOT TRY . . .
The Hitchhiker's Guide to the Galaxy (2005)
Idiocracy (2006)

DID YOU KNOW?
Douglas Rain lent his voice to HAL 9000 in Stanley Kubrick's *2001: a Space Odyssey*, made in 1968, and can be heard again here as the malevolent computer.

Some Like It Hot

CERTIFICATE: **U** | YEAR: **1959** | COUNTRY: **US** | **BW** | RUNNING TIME: **121 MINUTES**

SYNOPSIS

Chicago, 1929: when two underemployed musicians witness a St Valentine's Day massacre, they nearly become victims themselves. Their only escape from mobster Spats Columbo is to join a jazz band heading for Florida, but there's a problem – it's an all-girl orchestra with a knockout vocalist.

REVIEW

Tony Curtis and Jack Lemmon are ideally matched in this crackling comedy, as the 1920s musicians who join an all-girl band to escape the Mob. Yet, amazingly, Billy Wilder had originally wanted Bob Hope and Danny Kaye, and even considered casting Frank Sinatra instead of Lemmon (Lemmon went on to win a Bafta). Curtis didn't always get along with Marilyn Monroe (in her first picture in two years) and compared their embraces to kissing Hitler (ironically, the name she gave the bullying Wilder). Yet despite traumas in her personal life, Monroe was never better as she falls for Curtis's bogus oil tycoon (he boasts the voice of Cary Grant), and Lemmon's fling with his own eccentric millionaire is, if anything, even more hilarious. Clearly, the personality clashes both on- and off-screen were crucial to this becoming a true film classic, for, as Joe E Brown famously says in the last line, "Nobody's perfect!"

DAVID PARKINSON

QUOTE UNQUOTE

Will you look at that. Look how she moves! It's like Jell-O on springs. Must have some sort of built-in motor or something. I tell you – it's a whole different sex! JERRY

IF YOU ENJOYED THIS, WHY NOT TRY ...

Mrs Doubtfire (1993)
Tootsie (1982)

CAST

Marilyn Monroe *Sugar Kane* • Tony Curtis *Joe/Josephine* • Jack Lemmon *Jerry/Daphne* • George Raft *Spats Columbo* • Pat O'Brien *Mulligan* • Joe E Brown *Osgood E Fielding III* • Nehemiah Persoff *Little Bonaparte* • Joan Shawlee *Sweet Sue* • Billy Gray *Sig Poliakoff*

DIRECTOR

Billy Wilder

SCREENPLAY

Billy Wilder, IAL Diamond, from the film *Fanfares of Love* by Robert Thoeren, M Logan

AWARDS

Academy Awards (1): Costume Design (black and white)
Baftas (1): Foreign Actor (Jack Lemmon)

DVD EXTRAS

Special Edition: *Look Back* documentary; *Memories from the Sweet Sue's* featurette; virtual hall of memories; original press book gallery; theatrical trailer; other Billy Wilder film trailers.

DID YOU KNOW?

After Jerry Lewis turned down Jack Lemmon's lead role, he was regularly sent flowers by Lemmon with the message: "Thanks for being an idiot."

Sons of the Desert

CERTIFICATE: **U** | YEAR: **1933** | COUNTRY: **US** | **BW** | RUNNING TIME: **64 MINUTES**

SYNOPSIS

Married men Stan and Ollie pledge to attend a special meeting of "Sons of the Desert" – their fraternity lodge – in Chicago, but Ollie's wife forbids him to attend. The boys pretend to take a cruise to Honolulu for their health, but their wellbeing is put at risk when the lie starts to unravel.

REVIEW

This is probably the finest and fastest Laurel and Hardy feature film, in which Stan and Ollie attempt to con their intimidating wives (played by the wonderful Mae Busch and Dorothy Christy) with a story about a recuperative ocean cruise so they can attend the Chicago convention of their fraternity lodge (the Sons of the Desert of the title). The ridiculous men-only antics of the lodge are brilliantly exploited, especially by the bumptious Charley Chase, and the convoluted plot is a masterpiece of slapstick invention. Highlights include Ollie flirting on the phone while not realising he's talking to his wife, the wax fruit sequence and the send-up of Busby Berkeley with the hula dancers. The international society devoted to all Stan and Ollie's works bears the name of this film – an indication of how highly it is regarded. **TOM HUTCHINSON**

CAST

Stan Laurel *Stan* • Oliver Hardy *Ollie* • Charley Chase • Mae Busch *Mrs Lottie Chase Hardy* • Dorothy Christy *Mrs Betty Laurel*

DIRECTOR

William A Seiter

SCREENPLAY

Frank Craven, Byron Morgan

DVD EXTRAS

Laurel and Hardy Volume 13: colourised version of the main feature; three shorts: *We Faw Down; The Purple Moment; On the Wrong Trek*.

QUOTE UNQUOTE

Well, here's another nice mess you've gotten me into. OLLIE

IF YOU ENJOYED THIS, WHY NOT TRY . . .

Let's Do It Again (1975)
Their First Mistake (1932)

DID YOU KNOW?

Although this is B-movie length, it made more money than most of the features that year, coming in the top ten at the box office.

Strictly Ballroom

CERTIFICATE: **PG** | YEAR: **1992** | COUNTRY: **AUS** | **COLOUR** | RUNNING TIME: **90 MINUTES**

SYNOPSIS

The staid world of regional ballroom dancing in Australia is scandalised when Scott Hastings becomes determined to break with tradition and devise his own steps. His maverick attitude alienates those closest to him and only dowdy beginner Fran is willing to help him perform his exciting choreography.

REVIEW

Writer/director Baz Luhrmann drew on his rural Australian roots for his bright, breezy and strictly fabulous feature debut, which delves into the insular world of regional ballroom dancing. Paul Mercurio plays the rebel ballroom star who hesitantly teams up with ugly duckling novice Tara Morice for an important contest in which he plans to perform his own Latin routine rather than the boring steps set by the conservative dancing federation. Will love be in the air? What do you think! As kitsch and as corny as anything, this hilarious and heart-warming crowd-pleaser is an exuberant joy from sequined start to feathered finish. A calling card for Luhrmann's singularly eccentric style, this first film in his "Red Curtain Trilogy" (completed by (*William Shakespeare's Romeo + Juliet* and *Moulin Rouge!*) put him firmly on the international map.
ALAN JONES

CAST

Paul Mercurio *Scott Hastings* • Tara Morice *Fran* • Bill Hunter *Barry Fife* • Pat Thomson *Shirley Hastings* • Gia Carides *Liz Holt* • Peter Whitford *Les Kendall* • Barry Otto *Doug Hastings* • John Hannan *Ken Railings* • Sonia Kruger *Tina Sparkle*

DIRECTOR

Baz Luhrmann

SCREENPLAY

Baz Luhrmann, Craig Pearce, from a story by Luhrmann, Andrew Bovell, from an original idea by Luhrmann and the NIDA stage production

AWARDS

Baftas (3): Production Design, Costume Design, Original Score

DVD EXTRAS

Collector's Edition: behind-the-scenes featurette; John Paul *Young Love Is in the Air* music video; cast biographies. Also available on Blu-ray.

CONTENT ADVICE

Contains swearing.

QUOTE UNQUOTE

Where do you think we'd be if everyone went around making up their own steps? **BARRY FIFE**

IF YOU ENJOYED THIS, WHY NOT TRY ...

Dirty Dancing (1987)
Footloose (1984)

DID YOU KNOW?

Baz Luhrmann had a set of rules that he used for his "Red Curtain" trilogy, dubbed "theatricalised cinema": 1) let the viewer know how the film will end within the first ten minutes; 2) set the action in a world of heightened reality; 3) keep the audience awake.

Veronica Lake's on the take

PRESTON STURGES'
SULLIVAN'S TRAVELS

Sullivan's Travels

CERTIFICATE: **PG** | YEAR: **1941** | COUNTRY: **US** | **BW** | RUNNING TIME: **86 MINUTES**

SYNOPSIS

Hollywood comedy director John L Sullivan has decided to make a serious film about the travails of the common man, and seeks to experience what it means to suffer by posing as a hobo. On his first, failed attempt to escape Hollywood, Sullivan meets a girl at a diner who offers to help him blend in.

REVIEW

This sparkling satire from writer/director Preston Sturges centres on the age-old Hollywood dilemma of art versus entertainment. Giving perhaps his best performance, Joel McCrea plays a hugely successful comedy director who's planning to make a serious movie called *O Brother, Where Art Thou?* (the Coen brothers paid homage to Sturges with their film of the same name in 2000). So he hits the road, disguised as a tramp, in an attempt to find out what it means to suffer. With Veronica Lake in a star-making turn as McCrea's travelling companion, the plot veers from inspired insight to corny contrivance at such a rattling pace, the sheer vigour of the action carries you along. This classic should leave you in no doubt where Sturges thought a movie's first duty lay, yet it's also one of the few films that manages to strike a winning balance between entertainment and conscience. **DAVID PARKINSON**

CAST

Joel McCrea *John L Sullivan* • Veronica Lake *The girl* • William Demarest *Mr Jones* • Robert Warwick *Mr Lebrand* • Franklin Pangborn *Mr Casalais* • Porter Hall *Mr Hadrian* • Robert Greig *Sullivan's butler* • Eric Blore *Sullivan's valet* • Arthur Hoyt *Preacher* • Preston Sturges *Man in film studio*

DIRECTOR

Preston Sturges

SCREENPLAY

Preston Sturges

QUOTE UNQUOTE

There's a lot to be said for making people laugh. Did you know that that's all some people have? **JOHN L SULLIVAN**

IF YOU ENJOYED THIS, WHY NOT TRY . . .

Easy Living (1937)
O Brother, Where Art Thou? (2000)

DID YOU KNOW?

Veronica Lake (who was pregnant throughout the shoot) sports her famous peek-a-boo hairstyle. However, the government asked her to cut it off to help the war effort, as so many female munitions workers kept getting their copycat hair caught in the machinery.

■

This Is Spinal Tap

CERTIFICATE: **15** | YEAR: **1984** | COUNTRY: **US** | **COLOUR** | RUNNING TIME: **79 MINUTES**

SYNOPSIS

Documentary film-maker Marty DiBergi follows the American comeback tour of Britain's most punctual heavy rockers, Spinal Tap, as they launch their provocative new album *Smell the Glove*. The Tap are back, but poor sales and backstage squabbles threaten the rock 'n' roll dream.

REVIEW

This brilliantly crafted and completely on-target satire of the rock 'n' roll industry is filmed in mock documentary style, with every rock-music cliché savagely lampooned for maximum hilarity. Director Rob Reiner (playing Marty DiBergi, whose name is a tribute to Martin Scorsese, Brian De Palma and Steven Spielberg rolled into one) follows a fictitious British heavy metal band on tour. The Stonehenge-inspired production number is a highlight, but there's also immense pleasure to be had in the details, particularly the unbelievably crass lyrics of songs like *Big Bottom* and *Sex Farm*. Christopher Guest and Michael McKean are perfect as the group's incredibly stupid lead guitarist and singer, and Reiner's unsurpassed spoof never hits a false note. This pop send-up landmark has deservedly become a cult classic. **ALAN JONES**

CAST

Christopher Guest *Nigel Tufnel (lead guitar)* • Michael McKean *David St Hubbins (lead guitar)* • Harry Shearer *Derek Smalls (bass)* • RJ Parnell *Mick Shrimpton (drums)* • David Kaff *Viv Savage (keyboards)* • Rob Reiner *Marti DiBergi* • Bruno Kirby *Tommy Pischedda* • Anjelica Huston *Designer* • Billy Crystal *Mime artist* • Patrick Macnee *Sir Denis Eaton-Hogg*

DIRECTOR

Rob Reiner

SCREENPLAY

Christopher Guest, Michael McKean, Harry Shearer, Rob Reiner

DVD EXTRAS

Special Edition: commentary by Spinal Tap; interview with Rob Reiner; never-before-seen footage; out-takes; *Catching up with Marti DiBergi*; theatrical trailer; four music videos; six TV commercials; flower people press conference. Also available on Blu-ray.

CONTENT ADVICE

Contains swearing.

QUOTE UNQUOTE

The numbers all go to eleven. Look, right across the board, eleven, eleven, eleven and... **NIGEL TUFNEL**

IF YOU ENJOYED THIS, WHY NOT TRY ...

Anvil: the Story of Anvil (2008)
A Mighty Wind (2003)

DID YOU KNOW?

Several punters approached director Rob Reiner when the film opened and said they loved it, but he should have picked a better known band for his documentary.

Tootsie

CERTIFICATE: **15** | YEAR: **1982** | COUNTRY: **US** | **COLOUR** | RUNNING TIME: **111 MINUTES**

SYNOPSIS

Middle-aged actor Michael Dorsey is struggling to find employment because of his reputation for being difficult to work with. In desperation, he decides to attend an audition he has coached a friend for and is delighted to land the role – as a mature woman in a popular hospital-set soap opera.

REVIEW

One of the highlights of Dustin Hoffman's illustrious career, this cross-dressing comedy drama avoids all the obvious pitfalls and manages to make some pertinent comments about the role of women within both showbiz and society. Hoffman's Dorothy Michaels, the alter ego in drag that struggling actor Michael Dorsey resorts to when all conventional attempts to gain work have failed, is a wonderfully realised creation. And she's also a testament to Hoffman's painstaking preparation for the part – as practice, he read the role of Blanche DuBois from *A Streetcar Named Desire* to friend Meryl Streep. Director Sydney Pollack judges the shifts of tone to perfection, but special mention should be made of his clever pastiche of daytime soaps. Nominated for ten Oscars, the film landed only one – a best supporting statuette for Jessica Lange, who pipped co-star Teri Garr to the award. **DAVID PARKINSON**

CAST

Dustin Hoffman *Michael Dorsey/ Dorothy Michaels* • Jessica Lange *Julie* • Teri Garr *Sandy* • Dabney Coleman *Ron* • Charles Durning *Les* • Bill Murray *Jeff* • Sydney Pollack *George Fields* • George Gaynes *John Van Horn* • Geena Davis *April*

DIRECTOR

Sydney Pollack

SCREENPLAY

Larry Gelbart, Murray Schisgal, Elaine May (uncredited), from a story by Don McGuire, Gelbart

AWARDS

Academy Awards (1): Supporting Actress (Jessica Lange)
Baftas (2): Actor (Dustin Hoffman), Make-up

DVD EXTRAS

Anniversary Edition: *A Better Man* – the making of Tootsie; deleted scenes; Dustin Hoffman screen test footage.

QUOTE UNQUOTE

Look, you don't know me from Adam. But I was a better man with you as a woman than I ever was with a woman as a man. Know what I mean? **MICHAEL DORSEY**

IF YOU ENJOYED THIS, WHY NOT TRY ...

Some Like It Hot (1959)
Victor/Victoria (1982)

DID YOU KNOW?

Dustin Hoffman used an oscilloscope to attune his vocal chords to a female wave pattern for his cross-dressing role. At first, he could only achieve a credible falsetto in a French accent, but eventually discovered that a Deep South accent worked as well.

Toy Story & Toy Story 2

CERTIFICATE: **PG/U** | YEAR: **1995/1999** | COUNTRY: **US** | **COLOUR** | RUNNING TIME: **88 MINUTES**

SYNOPSIS

These animated adventures begin with pullstring cowboy toy Woody and brash, state-of-the-art space ranger Buzz Lightyear as bitter rivals, battling for the affection of their young owner. By the sequel, the toys are fast friends, and when Woody gets stolen, it's Buzz Lightyear to the rescue.

REVIEW

These magnificent films restored credibility to that much debased term "family entertainment", the original making history as the first completely computer-generated animation feature. In both, director John Lasseter delivers great stories that not only entertain children but can also be enjoyed as jokey parables by adults. They concern the adventures of pullstring cowboy Woody (Tom Hanks), who has his position as his owner's favourite toy usurped by the arrival of hi-tech space-ranger Buzz Lightyear (Tim Allen). In the sequel, Woody is stolen by a sleazy toy collector and Buzz mounts a rescue mission. Apart from the brilliant characterisations of Hanks, Allen and the rest of the cast, mention should also be made of Randy Newman's Oscar-nominated music and songs *You've Got a Friend* and *When She Loved Me*, which provide a perfect complement to the action. **TOM HUTCHINSON/DAVID PARKINSON**

QUOTE UNQUOTE

To infinity... and beyond! **BUZZ LIGHTYEAR**

IF YOU ENJOYED THIS, WHY NOT TRY ...

Monsters, Inc (2001)
Toy Story 3 (2010)

■

CAST

Tom Hanks *Woody* • Tim Allen *Buzz Lightyear* • Joan Cusack *Jessie* • Kelsey Grammer *Prospector* • Don Rickles *Mr Potato Head* • Jim Varney *Slinky Dog* • Wallace Shawn *Rex* • John Ratzenberger *Hamm* • John Morris *Andy* • Laurie Metcalf *Andy's mom* • R Lee Ermey *Sarge* • Jodi Benson *Barbie* • Annie Potts *Bo Peep*

DIRECTOR

John Lasseter, Lee Unkrich, Ash Brannon

SCREENPLAY

Joss Whedon, Andrew Stanton, Joel Cohen, Alec Sokolow, Rita Hsiao, Doug Chamberlin, Chris Webb

AWARDS

Academy Awards (Toy Story) (1): Special Achievement Award (John Lasseter)

DVD EXTRAS

The Ultimate Toy Box (3 discs): *Toy Story*: making-of documentary; *Tin Toy* - animated short; trailer for *Monsters Inc*; *Toy Story 2*: *Luxo Junior* - animated short; *Woody's Round Up* music video; *Coolest Toy* - featurette; character featurette; out takes; Bonus disc: Introductions by film-makers; *The History of Toy Story*; character design; deleted scenes; music videos; TV commercials; hidden jokes; posters; trailers; featurettes covering storyboard, location, music, sound and animation production.

DID YOU KNOW?

Director John Lasseter created Buzz Lightyear in his own likeness - they share similar eyebrows, cheekbones and even dimpled chins.

Trading Places

CERTIFICATE: **15** | YEAR: **1983** | COUNTRY: **US** | **COLOUR** | RUNNING TIME: **111 MINUTES**

SYNOPSIS

Millionaire businessmen Mortimer and Randolph Duke frame their nephew Louis, a conceited stockbroker in their own firm, for theft and drugs, and replace him with conman Billy Ray Valentine. Favouring nurture over nature, Mortimer bets that Valentine will make good while Louis turns to crime.

REVIEW

This blatant, unacknowledged reworking of *The Prince and the Pauper* is a rattling comedy showcase for the unique talents of Eddie Murphy and Dan Aykroyd, who have seldom recaptured the form they show here. However, there's no question that the acting honours go to veterans Don Ameche and Ralph Bellamy, as the mischievous business bigwigs whose wager brings about the respective rise and fall of a lowlife conman (Murphy) and a pompous broker (Aykroyd). Jamie Lee Curtis also makes quite an impression as a kind-hearted hooker and proved that there was more to her than screaming and running away from slash-happy psychopaths. Director John Landis tends to pull his satirical punches against yuppiedom, and it's a shame that he settles for a brash slapstick finale after so many fresh, immaculately timed comic situations, but this remains very entertaining. **DAVID PARKINSON**

QUOTE UNQUOTE

When I was growing up, if we wanted a Jacuzzi, we had to fart in the tub. **BILLY RAY VALENTINE**

IF YOU ENJOYED THIS, WHY NOT TRY ...
Brewster's Millions (1985)
The Sting (1973)

CAST

Eddie Murphy *Billy Ray Valentine* • Dan Aykroyd *Louis Winthorpe III* • Jamie Lee Curtis *Ophelia* • Ralph Bellamy *Randolph Duke* • Don Ameche *Mortimer Duke* • Denholm Elliott *Coleman* • Paul Gleason *Beeks* • Bo Diddley *Pawnbroker* • Jim Belushi [James Belushi] *King Kong*

DIRECTOR

John Landis

SCREENPLAY

Timothy Harris, Herschel Weingrod

AWARDS

Baftas (2): Supporting Actor (Denholm Elliott), Supporting Actress (Jamie Lee Curtis)

DVD EXTRAS

Special Collector's Edition: making-of feature; *Dressing the Part*; deleted scenes; trading stories.

CONTENT ADVICE

Contains swearing, nudity.

DID YOU KNOW?

James Belushi makes an early appearance in the film during the train scene in which he is dressed in a gorilla suit.

The Truman Show

CERTIFICATE: **PG** | YEAR: **1998** | COUNTRY: **US** | **COLOUR** | RUNNING TIME: **98 MINUTES**

SYNOPSIS

Truman Burbank leads an idyllic life in a perfect town. But what he doesn't know is that, since birth, his every move has been part of an intricately orchestrated reality television show and his "world" is an elaborate set. When cracks in the illusion appear, Truman sets out to find the truth.

REVIEW

Scripted by director/screenwriter Andrew Niccol and flawlessly executed by director Peter Weir, this ingenious satire about media omnipotence is both dazzling and sophisticated from audacious start to poignant finale. In a role that reveals his dramatic range, Jim Carrey plays Truman Burbank, star of the world's most popular reality TV show, although he doesn't know it. Burbank thinks he lives in the idyllic island community of Seahaven, but it's just a set housed in a vast studio, and all his family and friends are actors. How that realisation slowly dawns and spurs him on to find out what's real and what's fake in his emotionally confused universe is the stuff of ambitious cinematic brilliance. Carrey gives a suitably restrained performance, and he receives superlative support from Ed Harris (as the programme's creator, Christof) and Laura Linney (as Truman's "wife", Meryl). **ALAN JONES**

CAST

Jim Carrey *Truman Burbank* • Ed Harris *Christof* • Laura Linney *Meryl* • Noah Emmerich *Marlon* • Natascha McElhone *Lauren/Sylvia* • Holland Taylor *Truman's mother* • Brian Delate *Truman's father*

DIRECTOR

Peter Weir

SCREENPLAY

Andrew Niccol

AWARDS

Baftas (3): Director, Original Screenplay, Production Design

DVD EXTRAS

Special Collector's Edition: two-part making-of feature; visual effects feature; deleted scenes; outtakes; theatrical trailers; TV spots. Also available on Blu-ray.

QUOTE UNQUOTE

Good morning, and in case I don't see ya, good afternoon, good evening, and good night! **TRUMAN BURBANK**

IF YOU ENJOYED THIS, WHY NOT TRY ...

Edtv (1999)
Pleasantville (1998)

DID YOU KNOW?

The streets in Seahaven (Lancaster Plaza, Barrymore Road, DeMille Street) are all named after famous movie stars and directors, and Truman's surname, Burbank, is the California location of many of the classic Hollywood studios.

Wallace & Gromit in The Curse of the Were-Rabbit

CERTIFICATE: **U** | YEAR: **2005** | COUNTRY: **UK** | **COLOUR** | RUNNING TIME: **81 MINUTES**

SYNOPSIS

Business looks up for Wallace and Gromit's humane pest-control outfit when the home of animal-lover Lady Tottingham is invaded by rabbits. But then a mysterious beast starts destroying local gardens on the eve of the annual Giant Vegetable Competition, and they find their methods called into question.

REVIEW

Winner of the Oscar for best animated film, the first feature-length adventure for Nick Park's Claymation heroes sees the enterprising inventor (voiced, as ever, by veteran actor Peter Sallis) and his faithful dog in the pest-control business, chasing an elusive monster that's causing havoc in their neighbourhood gardens. Despite being peppered slightly too heavily with modern innuendo, the tale retains its charm and gains plenty of comic mileage from its quaint depiction of northern life. Working-class Wallace's rivalry with trigger-happy toff Victor (voiced by Ralph Fiennes) and his tentative relationship with animal-loving aristocrat Lady Tottington (Helena Bonham Carter) are especially amusing, and there are some great references to classic horror movies. But it's facially expressive Gromit who steals the show, causing genuine hilarity without uttering a single word. **SLOAN FREER**

CAST

Peter Sallis *Wallace* • Ralph Fiennes *Victor Quartermaine* • Helena Bonham Carter *Lady Tottington* • Peter Kay *PC Mackintosh* • Liz Smith *Mrs Mulch* • Nicholas Smith *Reverend Clement Hedges*

DIRECTOR

Nick Park, Steve Box

SCREENPLAY

Nick Park, Bob Baker, Steve Box, Mark Burton, from characters created by Nick Park, Steve Rushton

AWARDS

Academy Awards (1): Animated Feature
Baftas (1): British Film

DVD EXTRAS

Two-disc edition: guide to stop-motion animation by Nick Park and Steve Box; nine deleted scenes; behind the scenes features including *A Day in the Life at Aardmann*; how the bunny figures were assembled featurette; short films: *Stage Fright* and three from the *Cracking Contraptions* series; production photographs of the sets and characters; DVD ROM featuring kids' creative activities.

QUOTE UNQUOTE

I'm sorry, Gromit. I know you're doing this for my own good, but the fact is I'm just crackers about cheese. **WALLACE**

IF YOU ENJOYED THIS, WHY NOT TRY...

A Close Shave (1995)
The Wrong Trousers (1993)

DID YOU KNOW?

The creator of Wallace & Gromit, Nick Park, admitted in an interview that he based Wallace on his own father, who was an "an incurable tinkerer". Among Park Sr's inventions was a combo beach hut and trailer, with full-sized furniture bolted to the floor.

Way Out West

CERTIFICATE: **U** | YEAR: **1937** | COUNTRY: **US** | **BW** | RUNNING TIME: **63 MINUTES**

SYNOPSIS

Stan and Ollie are heading west for Brushwood Gulch; their mission is to deliver the deeds of a goldmine to a deceased prospector's daughter. The pair are unable to keep the secret for long, however, and are soon swindled out of the document by an unscrupulous saloon owner and his showgirl wife.

REVIEW

In their most memorable full-length feature, Stan Laurel and Oliver Hardy get to sing their hit song *Trail of the Lonesome Pine* as they go west to deliver a mine-deed inheritance to prospector's daughter Rosina Lawrence. However, they are waylaid by crooked saloon owner James Finlayson (in one of his earliest appearances with Stan and Ollie) and his moll, Sharon Lynne. At various stages called *You'd Be Surprised*, *Tonight's the Night* and *In the Money*, this inspired western parody contains some of the duo's most celebrated routines (with several other funny scenes ending up on the cutting room floor to keep the action around the customary B-movie length of one hour). In a marvellous tribute to 1934's *It Happened One Night*, Ollie can be seen flagging down a coach by flashing his leg. One of those films you can watch umpteen times and still come back for more. **DAVID PARKINSON**

CAST
Stan Laurel *Stan* • Oliver Hardy *Ollie* • James Finlayson *Mickey Finn* • Sharon Lynne *Lola Marcel* • Rosina Lawrence *Mary Roberts* • Stanley Fields *Sheriff*

DIRECTOR
James W Horne

SCREENPLAY
Charles Rogers, Felix Adler, James Parrott, from a story by Jack Jevne, Charles Rogers

DVD EXTRAS
Laurel and Hardy Volume 3: colourised version of main feature; b&w and colourised versions of two shorts: *One Good Turn, Thicker than Water*.

QUOTE UNQUOTE
A lot of weather we've been having lately! OLLIE

IF YOU ENJOYED THIS, WHY NOT TRY ...
Cat Ballou (1965)
Go West (1925)

DID YOU KNOW?
The Simpsons creator Matt Groening has said that one of the most repeated catchphrases from the series (Homer's "Doh!") was inspired by James Finlayson's use of the exclamation in this film and others.

What's Up, Doc?

CERTIFICATE: **U** | YEAR: **1972** | COUNTRY: **US** | **COLOUR** | RUNNING TIME: **90 MINUTES**

SYNOPSIS

Four identical suitcases containing, variously, clothes, state secrets, jewels and musical rocks, get mixed up in a San Francisco hotel, sparking a series of crazy events that engulf shy musicologist Howard Bannister, who's also being pursued by grifter Judy Maxwell, for whom it's love at first sight.

REVIEW

Barbra Streisand stars as the zany college dropout with her eyes on absent-minded music professor Ryan O'Neal in this hilarious homage to the 1930s screwball comedies of Howard Hawks and Preston Sturges from director Peter Bogdanovich. The tone is set by the wacky title, a reference to the scene when eccentric Streisand meets shy O'Neal for the first time – she's chomping on a carrot à la Bugs Bunny – and the plot revolves around the mix up of four sets of identical tartan luggage. There's brilliant support from Madeline Kahn (in her first major role) as O'Neal's fiancée and Randy Quaid (a Bogdanovich regular who made his debut in *The Last Picture Show*), beautiful photography from Laszlo Kovacs and a climactic car chase through the streets of San Francisco that's guaranteed to take your breath away. It's a shame that Bogdanovich has never again touched these heights of cartoonish wit.

TOM HUTCHINSON

CAST

Barbra Streisand *Judy Maxwell* • Ryan O'Neal *Professor Howard Bannister* • Madeline Kahn *Eunice Burns* • Kenneth Mars *Hugh Simon* • Austin Pendleton *Frederick Larrabee* • Michael Murphy *Mr Smith* • Phil Roth *Mr Jones* • Sorrell Booke *Harry* • Stefan Gierasch *Fritz* • Mabel Albertson *Mrs Van Hoskins* • Liam Dunn *Judge Maxwell* • Randall R "Randy" Quaid [Randy Quaid] *Professor Hosquith*

DIRECTOR

Peter Bogdanovich

SCREENPLAY

Buck Henry, David Newman, from a story by Peter Bogdanovich

QUOTE UNQUOTE

I know I'm different, but from now on I'm going to try and be the same. **JUDY MAXWELL**

IF YOU ENJOYED THIS, WHY NOT TRY ...

Bringing Up Baby (1938)
You Can't Take It with You (1938)

DID YOU KNOW?

"Love means never having to say you're sorry" was the key line from *Love Story*, starring Ryan O'Neal. Yet when Barbra Streisand says it to him in *What's Up, Doc?*, he says: "That's the dumbest thing I ever heard."

When Harry Met Sally...

CERTIFICATE: **15** | YEAR: **1989** | COUNTRY: **US** | **COLOUR** | RUNNING TIME: **91 MINUTES**

SYNOPSIS

Harry Burns reckons "men and women can't be friends because the sex part always gets in the way". Initially, Sally Albright doesn't agree with him about this or anything else. But as their paths repeatedly cross over the years, the mismatched couple see their views, and friendship, evolve.

REVIEW

Essentially concerned with the several meetings and partings of two college graduates over a decade or so, as life and love take their toll, this romantic comedy argues the question whether men and women can ever have friendship without sex. In truth, the movie, with its glitzy New York locations and beguiling soundtrack of popular standards, offers a cutesy, superficial and glamorised excursion into Woody Allen territory, but triumphs nevertheless as expert and irresistible escapist entertainment. The teaming of Meg Ryan and Billy Crystal is perfect, while supporting stars Carrie Fisher and Bruno Kirby are outstanding and add a welcome suggestion of edge. The fake-orgasm-in-a-deli set piece propelled Ryan into stratospheric stardom, but there are numerous other pleasures to be found in Nora Ephron's Oscar-nominated screenplay and Rob Reiner's astute direction. **ROBIN KARNEY**

CAST

Billy Crystal *Harry Burns* • Meg Ryan *Sally Albright* • Carrie Fisher *Marie* • Bruno Kirby *Jess* • Steven Ford *Joe* • Lisa Jane Persky *Alice*

DIRECTOR

Rob Reiner

SCREENPLAY

Nora Ephron

AWARDS

Baftas (1): Best Original Screenplay

DVD EXTRAS

Making-of documentary; commentary by Rob Reiner; seven deleted scenes; Harry Connick *It Had to Be You* music video; theatrical trailer.

CONTENT ADVICE

Contains swearing.

QUOTE UNQUOTE

I'll have what she's having. **WOMAN IN RESTAURANT**

IF YOU ENJOYED THIS, WHY NOT TRY ...

Reality Bites (1994)
Sleepless in Seattle (1993)

DID YOU KNOW?

In one scene, Harry is seen reading Stephen King's *Misery*. Rob Reiner's definitive version of that bestseller was released in cinemas the following year.

Withnail & I

CERTIFICATE: **15** | YEAR: **1986** | COUNTRY: **UK** | **COLOUR** | RUNNING TIME: **102 MINUTES**

SYNOPSIS

In 1969, two out-of-work actors in poor physical and mental shape eke out an existence in their cold and run-down north London flat. When the penniless pair pay Withnail's wealthy, eccentric uncle a visit, they obtain the keys to his country cottage for what turns out to be an eventful weekend.

REVIEW

This great little film launched the career of Richard E Grant and has since developed into a cult classic. Grant and Paul McGann play two dissolute actors living in a far-from-swinging London who are slowly unravelling under the pressures of obscurity and determined substance abuse. Tiring of the baroque squalor of their Camden flat, they decamp to a cottage in the Lake District ("We've gone on holiday by mistake") where they struggle to survive the weather and the lecherous Uncle Monty (the wonderful Richard Griffiths). There are memorable supporting turns along the way from Ralph Brown as a philosophising drug dealer and Michael Elphick as a sinister poacher. Hilarious, poignant and endlessly quotable (not least Grant's boozy tirade in a quiet tea room), this was written and directed by Bruce Robinson and based on his own experiences as a struggling actor. SUE HEAL

CAST

Richard E Grant *Withnail* • Paul McGann ... *and I* • Richard Griffiths *Monty* • Ralph Brown *Danny* • Michael Elphick *Jake* • Daragh O'Malley *Irishman* • Michael Wardle *Isaac Parkin* • Una Brandon-Jones *Mrs Parkin* • Noel Johnson *General*

DIRECTOR

Bruce Robinson

SCREENPLAY

Bruce Robinson

DVD EXTRAS

20th Anniversary Two-disc Edition: commentary by Bruce Robinson; commentary by Paul McGann, Ralph Brown; *Withnail and Us*, a 1999 documentary about the making of the film; behind the scenes stills by Ralph Steadman; the *Withnail & I* drinking game; "Swear-a-thon" feature; theatrical trailer; bonus CD of the original soundtrack. Also available on Blu-ray.

CONTENT ADVICE

Contains swearing, drug abuse.

QUOTE UNQUOTE

We want the finest wines available to humanity. And we want them here, and we want them now! WITHNAIL

IF YOU ENJOYED THIS, WHY NOT TRY ...

How to Get Ahead in Advertising (1989)
My Favorite Year (1982)

■

DID YOU KNOW?

In *Withnail & I*, Richard E Grant thought he was going to drink water in the scene where he supposedly gulps down a can of lighter fluid, but director Bruce Robinson had filled the can with vinegar to get a more realistic facial expression from the star.

Young Frankenstein

CERTIFICATE: **15** | YEAR: **1974** | COUNTRY: **US** | **BW** | RUNNING TIME: **101 MINUTES**

SYNOPSIS

Shamed medical-school teacher Frederick Frankenstein travels to Transylvania to inherit his infamous grandfather's castle. Following the discovery of a journal entitled "How I Did It" in the castle's library, he feels inspired to repeat his ancestor's experiments and reanimate the dead.

REVIEW

This loopy send-up of classic chiller clichés from Universal's monster heyday is one of director Mel Brooks's best comedies, and it's also one of the genre's most thorough and successful fright film parodies. Gene Wilder plays the infamous baron's grandson, who copies his ancestor's experiments only to create the singularly inane Peter Boyle. Filmed in sumptuous black and white, and shot on sets used in the 1931 original *Frankenstein*, Brooks's ingenious tribute is often hysterically funny and always a scream. Madeleine Kahn's "bride", Gene Hackman's blind hermit, Marty Feldman's hunchbacked Igor and the marvellous "Putting on the Ritz" musical number add to the fun and give this loving homage real staying power. And for those with eagle eyes: the gargoyle on the wall by the basement stairs was modelled on the director. **ALAN JONES**

CAST

Gene Wilder *Doctor Frederick Frankenstein* • Peter Boyle *Monster* • Marty Feldman *Igor* • Madeline Kahn *Elizabeth* • Cloris Leachman *Frau Blücher* • Teri Garr *Inga* • Kenneth Mars *Inspector Kemp* • Gene Hackman *Blindman* • Richard Haydn *Herr Falkstein*

DIRECTOR

Mel Brooks

SCREENPLAY

Gene Wilder, Mel Brooks, from characters created by Mary Shelley

DVD EXTRAS

Special Edition: commentary by Mel Brooks; behind-the-scenes documentary; out-takes; bloopers; deleted scenes; TV spots; theatrical trailers.

CONTENT ADVICE

Contains violence, swearing.

QUOTE UNQUOTE

Pardon me, boy. Is this the Transylvania station?
DR FREDERICK FRANKENSTEIN

IF YOU ENJOYED THIS, WHY NOT TRY . . .

Carry On Screaming (1966)
The Rocky Horror Picture Show (1975)

■

DID YOU KNOW?

Steve Tyler of Aerosmith wrote the band's hit *Walk This Way* after watching the film and seeing Marty Feldman's "Walk this way... this way" shenanigans. And to think Mel Brooks considered the joke too silly to keep in.

ZOOLANDER

Zoolander

CERTIFICATE: **12** | YEAR: **2001** | COUNTRY: **US/GER/AUS** | **COLOUR** | RUNNING TIME: **85 MINUTES**

SYNOPSIS

Derek Zoolander, the vain, self-absorbed king of the male-modelling world is under siege. Rival model Hansel may pinch his crown and a top designer has brainwashed Derek into assassinating an eminent statesman whose proposed new child-labour laws will spell disaster for the fashion industry.

REVIEW

This rapier-sharp satire on the fashion industry from director/star Ben Stiller balances hipness and endearing stupidity with expert precision. Based on a persona Stiller created for a fashion awards ceremony in 1996, Derek Zoolander is the king of the male-modelling world thanks to his "blue steel" stare. When he loses his title to new boy Hansel (Owen Wilson) and decides to retire, furtive fashion mogul Mugatu (Will Ferrell) comes to his rescue, only to brainwash the foolish fop into assassinating the Prime Minister of Malaysia who plans to outlaw sweatshops. Brilliantly conceived and executed, it mercilessly exposes the shallow and bitchy world of *haute couture*. Highlights include the catwalk duel between Zoolander and Hansel – as refereed by David Bowie – and the return home to his butch coal-mining family presided over by Jon Voight. **ALAN JONES**

CAST

Ben Stiller *Derek Zoolander* • Owen Wilson *Hansel* • Will Ferrell *Mugatu* • Christine Taylor *Matilda Jeffries* • Milla Jovovich *Katinka* • Jerry Stiller *Maury Ballstein* • Jon Voight *Larry Zoolander* • David Duchovny *JP Prewitt* • Anne Meara *Protestor*

DIRECTOR

Ben Stiller

SCREENPLAY

Drake Sather, Ben Stiller, John Hamburg, from a story by Sather, Stiller

DVD EXTRAS

Commentary by Ben Stiller, Drake Sather and John Hamburg; five deleted scenes with Ben Stiller commentary; five extended scenes with Ben Stiller commentary; out-takes; skits from the VH1/Vogue Fashion Awards; promotional spots' alternative end titles. Also available on Blu-ray.

QUOTE UNQUOTE

I'm pretty sure there's a lot more to life than being really, really, ridiculously good looking. **DEREK ZOOLANDER**

IF YOU ENJOYED THIS, WHY NOT TRY . . .

Pret-a-Porter (1994)
Tropic Thunder (2008)

DID YOU KNOW?

Not content with providing showbiz buddies like David Bowie and Winona Ryder with cameos as themselves, Ben Stiller also found roles for his parents, Jerry Stiller and Anne Meara, wife Christine Taylor, sister Amy and brother-in-law Mitch Winston.

Woody Allen: New York Storeys

VISITING NEW YORK FOR THE FIRST TIME IS always a thrill for the movie fan. I remember, in exquisite detail, my maiden voyage in 1990: bouncing down the Van Wyck Expressway from JFK airport in the type of yellow cab I'd seen so many times on screen; crossing into Manhattan via what must have been the Triborough Bridge, in constant awe as the skyscrapers rose up and swallowed us; marvelling at the criss-crossing traffic so familiar from so many movies; counting off the intersecting north-south avenues, Lexington, Madison, Broadway . . . But it was the unexpected sight of the Carnegie Deli, on 7th Avenue and 55th Street, with its vivid yellow sign, that provided my biggest jolt. This is the setting for Woody Allen's *Broadway Danny Rose* (one of an impressive five Allen films to reach the 100), whose story is told by a group of old-timers as they swap tall tales over even taller pastrami sandwiches.

As a lifelong lover of Allen's movies (the lion's share of which are set in Manhattan and, more importantly, shot in Manhattan), New York felt like my Mecca. Having watched *Broadway Danny Rose* more times than I'd care to recall, to glimpse the Carnegie Deli in colour was enough to turn my head. The film is shot in black and white, so I had not expected the yellow! And as you can see, I had to have my photograph taken standing outside.

Perhaps more than any film director, Allen has used the medium to map the avenues and alleyways of his home town. In the "affectionate immortalisation of a city" stakes, only Barry Levinson and John Waters come close, having repeatedly depicted the less iconic Baltimore where they both grew up – and perhaps Allen's hero, Ingmar Bergman, who shot a number of his key films on Faro Island in Sweden, where he latterly lived. But Allen's New York is surely the definitive portrait – it is *his* vision of the city that we want to exist, and it's one that's certainly more appealing to the tourist office than, say, Martin Scorsese's explorations of its underbelly in *Taxi Driver* and *Mean Streets*. Has anyone topped the love letter, both verbal and visual, that opens Allen's masterpiece *Manhattan*, with its besotted, black-and-white montage of landmarks such as Times Square, the Metropolitan Museum of Art and the Staten Island Ferry, all cut to the magnificent *Rhapsody in Blue*? (As Allen's narrator reflects, New York is a city that "existed in black and white and pulsated to the great *toons* of George Gershwin.")

He happens to love New York: Brooklyn-born Woody Allen amuses Diane Keaton with his theories on art in a scene from *Manhattan*. The film took in several of the city's museums, including the Metropolitan and the Museum of Modern Art

A CULTURALLY NOURISHING DAY COULD BE PLANNED exclusively around the museums, picturehouses and galleries that crop up in Allen's always urbane work: the aforementioned Metropolitan; the Guggenheim (also glimpsed in the *Manhattan* montage); the Hayden Planetarium (again *Manhattan*, where Woody and Diane Keaton dash to get out of the rain); the Thalia Cinema (now part of the Symphony Space centre) on the Upper West Side (where, in *Annie Hall*, he refuses to enter a showing of a Bergman film because it's already started); and on to the Belasco Theater on 44th Street (where the production in *Bullets over Broadway* is staged). Don't look for the Pageant second-hand bookstore in the East Village where Michael Caine and Barbara Hershey began their illicit affair in *Hannah and Her Sisters*, though – it's now a bar. Another warning: there's actually no bench at Riverview Terrace upon which to sit and re-create the famous sunrise image from the *Manhattan* poster,

with Woody and Diane looking out at the Queensboro Bridge. (A recurring disappointment, that – along with the fact that the New Yorker cinema, where in a fantasy sequence in *Annie Hall* Woody brings out media academic Marshall McLuhan to settle an argument in the queue, has been demolished.)

It's impractical to catalogue all of the locations preserved for posterity in the Woody Allen canon, but I like the fact that he shot much of *Hannah and Her Sisters* in his then-partner Mia Farrow's apartment on Central Park West – that's really working from home!

Mia Farrow and Dianne Wiest set Farrow's own table for a Thanksgiving dinner in *Hannah and Her Sisters*

A thorough search of the internet will furnish a long walking tour of Woody Allen's Manhattan, and you'll be able to stop off for a sturgeon blini at the Russian Tea Rooms (*Manhattan, New York Stories*) halfway. Do make a reservation, though – and remember that the often monochrome settings of the greatest comedy director's films will be in colour. **ANDREW COLLINS**

Ealing: the true home of comedy

THE UK'S CONTRIBUTION to screen comedy numbers a few towering individuals, such as Charlie Chaplin and Stan Laurel. Walworth-born Chaplin took his music-hall honed skills to Hollywood and became the king of silent comedy; native Lancastrian Laurel followed in his footsteps (literally: as a fellow member of Fred Karno's troupe, he once understudied the future Little Tramp) and went on to form a still unmatched partnership with Oliver Hardy. But, uniquely, the UK also gave the world of comedy a studio name to conjure with: Ealing, the home of films that

Native sons: Stan Laurel (far left, kneeling) and Charlie Chaplin (circled by the lifebelt) on their way to America as part of Fred Karno's vaudeville company

featured – in the words of producer Michael Balcon – "daydreamers, mild anarchists, little men who long to kick the boss in the teeth".

The studio began in a house in the London suburb of Ealing in 1902; in 1929, theatre producer Basil Dean formed Associated Radio (later Talking) Pictures and raised the cash for a new movie-making factory. The Ealing Studios we now know were completed in 1931, and soon forged a reputation with stars like Gracie Fields and George Formby.

But the comedic house style really emerged after Dean's departure, when Michael Balcon took over in 1938. His son, Jonathan Balcon, believes that it was his father's battles with bureaucracy that shaped what would universally be understood as Ealing Comedies: the little man with that burning desire to revolt.

Walter Forde's *Cheer Boys Cheer* (1939) is usually excluded from the classic canon. But its emphasis on a sense of community and traditional, artisan values (a small brewery stands up to an industrialised rival) instituted the Ealing trademarks that would raise spirits

The studios began when film pioneer Will Barker bought a house on Ealing Green in 1902. The structure was expanded by Basil Dean, and is still in use

National Service

Have You Chosen Your Job?
If Not
What About It?

Basil Radford eyes the contraband at the heart of Ealing's *Whisky Galore!* – one of the studio's classics that didn't quite make the 100

The many faces of Alec Guinness: the actor played all eight members of the D'Ascoyne family, including vigorous suffragette Lady Agatha, bluff military man General Rufus, the appropriately named Admiral Lord Horatio and man-of-the-cloth Lord Henry

in the depths of postwar austerity. Several more comedies produced under Balcon followed this template, but the Ealing Comedy brand is reserved for nine features: from Charles Crichton's *Hue and Cry* in 1947 to Charles Frend's *Barnacle Bill* in 1957 (both, incidentally, were scripted by the studio's most significant writer, TEB "Tibby" Clarke).

ALTHOUGH THE EALING COMEDIES ARE often viewed as a homogeneous whole, there's actually a pronounced difference between those penned by Tibby Clarke and those directed by Robert Hamer and Alexander Mackendrick. The latter pair tended towards an overtly subversive, almost cynical, tone, while Clarke emphasised community and co-operation.

In Clarke's *Passport to Pimlico* (1949, the earliest of Ealing's comedies to make the 100), Londoners are briefly tempted by the prospect of forming their own independent duchy of Burgundy. That they return is seen as an act of solidarity rather than a defeat. In *The Lavender Hill Mob* (1951), a mild-mannered bank clerk (played by Alec Guinness, pictured far left with fellow Ealing stalwart Stanley Holloway) turns criminal mastermind but is, inevitably but heart-breakingly, foiled. *The Titfield Thunderbolt* (1952) is perhaps Clarke's cosiest offering, centring on a rural train service, but it puts faith in community action and people above profit.

Things darkened significantly and deliciously with director Robert Hamer's *Kind Hearts and Coronets* (1949). Dastardly yet charismatic Louis Mazzini (Dennis Price) might just get away with murdering the snootily aristocratic members of the D'Ascoyne family (all eight of whom were memorably played by the chameleonic Alec Guinness), who slighted his mother and so deprived him of wealth and status. With

Alec Guinness's revolutionary invention is held back by the forces of self-interest in this brilliantly biting Ealing satire

Price's voiceover and Joan Greenwood's *femme fatale*, there's an almost thriller-like aura to the cynical action.

AMERICAN-BORN SCOT Alexander Mackendrick had even less time for class deference. He gleefully mocks the ruling elite as they try to prevent Hebridean islanders from salvaging contraband scotch in *Whisky Galore!* (1949), and exposes self-serving business moguls attempting to suppress an indestructible wonder fabric in *The Man in the White Suit* (1951). However, even the caustic Mackendrick softened occasionally, by allowing a canny Clyde skipper to trick an American tycoon into hiring his coal-powered tub in *The Maggie* (1953), and letting a dotty old dear profit from the in-fighting among a gang of dishonourable thieves in *The Ladykillers* (1955).

In 1955, the financially troubled studio was sold to the BBC and Balcon departed, with key creative personnel, to make *Barnacle Bill* at the MGM studios in Borehamwood. It was the last Ealing Comedy in name, if not spirit. Rivals filled the gap Ealing had left: Rank had the *Doctor* and *Carry On* series; British Lion boasted the exceptional talents of the Boulting Brothers, and Frank Launder and Sidney Gilliat. But none carried the resonance of the Ealing brand.

In 1988, Monty Python old boys John Cleese and Michael Palin teamed up with Charles Crichton and came pretty close to rediscovering the Ealing secret with *A Fish Called Wanda*, as did Bill Forsyth with 1983's *Local Hero*. But nothing will ever surpass the timeless originals.
DAVID PARKINSON   ■

The Beverly Hills mob: John Cleese and Jamie Lee Curtis put an Anglo-American spin on the Ealing style with *A Fish Called Wanda*

Titles by Decade

Directors

Contributors' Top Tens

DAVE ALDRIDGE
FREELANCE FILM WRITER
 1 Shaun of the Dead
 2 Bill & Ted's Bogus Journey*
 3 Man Bites Dog*
 4 Airplane!
 5 Galaxy Quest
 6 Fargo*
 7 Dr Strangelove, or How I
 Learned to Stop Worrying and
 Love the Bomb
 8 Sideways
 9 In Bruges*
 10 This Is Spinal Tap

JANE ANDERSON
RADIO EDITOR, RADIO TIMES
 1 This Is Spinal Tap
 2 Monty Python's Life of Brian
 3 Withnail & I
 4 Young Frankenstein
 5 Some Like It Hot
 6 The Producers
 7 Dr Strangelove, or How I
 Learned to Stop Worrying and
 Love the Bomb
 8 The Apartment
 9 The Raven*
 10 Toy Story

JEREMY ASPINALL
RADIO TIMES FILM UNIT
 1 Kind Hearts and Coronets
 2 Blazing Saddles
 3 Annie Hall
 4 National Lampoon's Animal
 House
 5 The Ladykillers
 6 Monty Python's Life of Brian
 7 Groundhog Day
 8 Midnight Run
 9 The Producers
 10 Dr Strangelove, or How I
 Learned to Stop Worrying and
 Love the Bomb

LUCY BARRICK
RADIO TIMES FILM UNIT
 1 This Is Spinal Tap
 2 The General

 3 Some Like It Hot
 4 The Cable Guy*
 5 The Producers
 6 The Jerk
 7 Ghost Busters
 8 Harold and Maude
 9 The Odd Couple
 10 Galaxy Quest

DAVID BUTCHER
DEPUTY TV EDITOR, RADIO TIMES
 1 The Philadelphia Story
 2 Dr Strangelove, or How I
 Learned to Stop Worrying and
 Love the Bomb
 3 The Jungle Book*
 4 The Incredibles*
 5 His Girl Friday
 6 Withnail & I
 7 Some Like It Hot
 8 Four Weddings and a Funeral
 9 The Jerk
 10 The Graduate

ANDREW COLLINS
FILM EDITOR, RADIO TIMES
 1 Monty Python and the Holy
 Grail
 2 This Is Spinal Tap
 3 Carry On Screaming
 4 Broadway Danny Rose
 5 The Music Box*
 6 Withnail & I
 7 Blazing Saddles
 7 The General
 9 The Ladykillers
 10 Lock, Stock and Two Smoking
 Barrels*

GILL CRAWFORD
WRITER, RADIO TIMES
 1 The Philadelphia Story
 2 Annie Hall
 3 The Graduate
 4 Bringing Up Baby
 5 It Happened One Night
 6 His Girl Friday
 7 Hannah and Her Sisters*
 8 Groundhog Day
 9 Four Weddings and a Funeral

 10 I Know Where I'm Going!*

GEOFF ELLIS
WRITER, RADIO TIMES
 1 The Producers
 2 Monty Python's Life of Brian
 3 Some Like It Hot
 4 A Night at the Opera
 5 It Happened One Night
 6 MASH
 7 Dr Strangelove, or How I
 Learned to Stop Worrying and
 Love the Bomb
 8 Toy Story
 9 Bringing Up Baby
 10 Airplane!

JOHN FERGUSON
FREELANCE FILM WRITER
 1 Raising Arizona
 2 Withnail & I
 3 The Royal Tenenbaums
 4 Sleeper
 5 Lost in Translation
 6 The Castle*
 7 Bad Santa*
 8 Airplane!
 9 The Man with Two Brains
 10 Monty Python's Life of Brian

TOM FOLLEY
RADIO TIMES FILM UNIT
 1 Some Like It Hot
 2 Toy Story 2
 3 Safety Last*
 4 The Philadelphia Story
 5 Withnail & I
 6 Groundhog Day
 7 Pleasantville
 8 Delicatessen*
 9 Four Weddings and a Funeral
 10 Heathers

SLOAN FREER
FREELANCE FILM WRITER
 1 Some Like It Hot
 2 Zoolander
 3 Lost in Translation
 4 Withnail & I

* not included in the 100

5 *Ninotchka*
6 *The Royal Tenenbaums*
7 *Bringing Up Baby*
8 *The Rocky Horror Picture Show**
9 *Addams Family Values**
10 *Love at First Bite**

RUPERT FROST
FREELANCE FILM WRITER

1 *Some Like It Hot*
2 *Kind Hearts and Coronets*
3 *The General*
4 *The Discreet Charm of the Bourgeoisie**
5 *Duck Soup*
6 *Dr Strangelove, or How I Learned to Stop Worrying and Love the Bomb*
7 *Manhattan*
8 *The Great Dictator*
9 *I'm All Right Jack*
10 *What's Up, Doc?*

JAMIE HEALY
RADIO TIMES FILM UNIT

1 *Monty Python's Life of Brian*
2 *The Big Lebowski*
3 *Trading Places*
4 *The Man with Two Brains*
5 *Withnail & I*
6 *Love and Death*
7 *Groundhog Day*
8 *This Is Spinal Tap*
9 *Ghost Busters*
10 *The Ladykillers*

ALAN JONES
FREELANCE FILM WRITER

1 *Some Like It Hot*
2 *Beyond the Valley of the Dolls**
3 *Pink Flamingos*
4 *Austin Powers: International Man of Mystery*
5 *This Is Spinal Tap*
6 *Shrek*
7 *Airplane!*
8 *Walk Hard: the Dewey Cox Story**
9 *Groundhog Day*
10 *Harold and Maude*

PAUL JONES
WRITER, *RADIOTIMES.COM*

1 *Ghost Busters*
2 *Office Space**
3 *How to Steal a Million**
4 *Withnail & I*
5 *Duck Soup*
6 *The Odd Couple*
7 *Une Femme Est une Femme**
8 *The Princess Bride**
9 *Bill & Ted's Excellent Adventure*
10 *Monty Python and the Holy Grail*

KAREN KRIZANOVICH
FREELANCE FILM WRITER

1 *Local Hero*
2 *The Man with Two Brains*
3 *Zoolander*
4 *Tropic Thunder**
5 *Big*
6 *Horse Feathers*
7 *His Girl Friday*
8 *Four Weddings and a Funeral*
9 *Airplane!*
10 *Kiss Kiss Bang Bang**

FRANCES LASS
WRITER, *RADIO TIMES*

1 *Monty Python's Life of Brian*
2 *This Is Spinal Tap*
3 *Leningrad Cowboys Go America*
4 *Shrek*
5 *Airplane!*
6 *Toy Story*
7 *Toy Story 2*
8 *A Mighty Wind**
9 *The Jerk*
10 *Blazing Saddles*

STUART MANNING
DESIGNER, *RADIO TIMES 100 GREATEST FILMS*

1 *Harold and Maude*
2 *Addams Family Values**
3 *Being There**
4 *Manhattan*
5 *The Opposite of Sex**
6 *The Fearless Vampire Killers**

7 *Amélie*
8 *Some Like It Hot*
9 *The Royal Tenenbaums*
10 *Little Miss Sunshine*

DAVID OPPEDISANO
WRITER, *RADIO TIMES*

1 *Bringing Up Baby*
2 *The Awful Truth*
3 *A New Leaf**
4 *His Girl Friday*
5 *It's a Gift**
6 *The Cheap Detective**
7 *Sleeper*
8 *The Philadelphia Story*
9 *Female Trouble*
10 *Midnight**

STELLA PAPAMICHAEL
FREELANCE FILM WRITER

1 *The Apartment*
2 *Raising Arizona*
3 *The Philadelphia Story*
4 *This Is Spinal Tap*
5 *Some Like It Hot*
6 *Sideways*
7 *When Harry Met Sally{ellipsis}*
8 *Dr Strangelove, or How I Learned to Stop Worrying and Love the Bomb*
9 *The Big Lebowski*
10 *Monty Python's Life of Brian*

DAVID PARKINSON
FREELANCE FILM WRITER

1 *Monsieur Hulot's Holiday*
2 *Monty Python's Life of Brian*
3 *A Hard Day's Night**
4 *The Music Box**
5 *This Is Spinal Tap*
6 *The Story of a Cheat**
7 *Gregory's Girl**
8 *The Rutles {--} All You Need Is Cash**
9 *Zelig**
10 *I'm All Right Jack*

BRIAN PENDREIGH
FREELANCE FILM WRITER

1 *Monty Python's Life of Brian*
2 *MASH*

3 *The Graduate*
4 *Groundhog Day*
5 *Sons of the Desert*
6 *Duck Soup*
7 *Blazing Saddles*
8 *A Fish Called Wanda*
9 *Being There**
10 *Local Hero*

TONY PETERS
RADIO TIMES FILM UNIT

1 *Annie Hall*
2 *This Is Spinal Tap*
3 *Some Like It Hot*
4 *A Night at the Opera*
5 *Monty Python and the Holy Grail*
6 *MASH*
7 *Love and Death*
8 *Tootsie*
9 *Young Frankenstein*
10 *Dr Strangelove, or How I Learned to Stop Worrying and Love the Bomb*

COLIN PRIOR
EDITOR, *RADIO TIMES 100 GREATEST FILMS*

1 *Toy Story*
2 *The Simpsons Movie**
3 *The Ladykillers*
4 *Shrek*
5 *Sideways*
6 *The Producers*
7 *One Hundred and One Dalmatians**
8 *Kind Hearts and Coronets*
9 *Trading Places*
10 *Mousehunt**

SUE ROBINSON
EDITOR, *RADIO TIMES 100 GREATEST FILMS*

1 *The Philadelphia Story*
2 *Monty Python's Life of Brian*
3 *Kind Hearts and Coronets*
4 *The General*
5 *Groundhog Day*
6 *Babe**
7 *A Night at the Opera*
8 *Galaxy Quest*
9 *Hot Fuzz**
10 *Tremors**

JAMIE RUSSELL
FREELANCE FILM WRITER

1 *Sons of the Desert*
2 *Horse Feathers*
3 *Dr Strangelove, or How I Learned to Stop Worrying and Love the Bomb*
4 *Duck Soup*
5 *Adaptation.*
6 *Borat: Cultural Learnings of America for Make Benefit Glorious Nation of Kazakhstan*
7 *Gentlemen Prefer Blondes*
8 *South Park: Bigger, Longer & Uncut**
9 *Monkey Business (1931)**
10 *Monty Python and the Holy Grail*

JACK SEALE
WRITER, *RADIO TIMES*

1 *The Royal Tenenbaums*
2 *Monty Python's Life of Brian*
3 *This Is Spinal Tap*
4 *Airplane!*

5 *The Apartment*
6 *Harold and Maude*
7 *Billy Liar*
8 *Withnail & I*
9 *Rushmore*
10 *The Naked Gun*

SUSANNAH STRAUGHAN
FREELANCE FILM WRITER

1 *This Is Spinal Tap*
2 *The Graduate*
3 *Kind Hearts and Coronets*
4 *Annie Hall*
5 *The Lady Eve*
6 *Sideways*
7 *The Big Lebowski*
8 *Being John Malkovich*
9 *Beyond the Valley of the Dolls**
10 *Office Space**

DAMON WISE
FREELANCE FILM WRITER

1 *Airplane II: the Sequel**
2 *Dodgeball: a True Underdog Story**
3 *Anchorman: the Legend of Ron Burgundy**
4 *Team America: World Police**
5 *School for Scoundrels**
6 *Office Space**
7 *The Boss of It All**
8 *Deuce Bigalow: European Gigolo**
9 *EuroTrip**
10 *Waiting for Guffman**